BUSINESS START-UPS
DONE DIRT CHEAP

BUSINESS START-UPS DONE DIRT CHEAP

◆

For entrepreneurs who want to minimize start-up costs and maximize chances of success

Bruce C. Thornton

iUniverse, Inc.
New York Lincoln Shanghai

BUSINESS START-UPS DONE DIRT CHEAP
For entrepreneurs who want to minimize start-up costs and maximize chances of success

iUniverse books may be ordered through booksellers or by contacting:

iUniverse
2021 Pine Lake Road, Suite 100
Lincoln, NE 68512
www.iuniverse.com
1-800-Authors (1-800-288-4677)

ISBN-13: 978-0-595-39262-9 (pbk)
ISBN-13: 978-0-595-83657-4 (ebk)
ISBN-10: 0-595-39262-8 (pbk)
ISBN-10: 0-595-83657-7 (ebk)

Printed in the United States of America

Contents

Acknowledgments

I owe much to my wife, Sharon, who shared (endured) every moment of our successes and failures, and to my long-term business partner, Dudley P. Warner, who is one of the most creative business development people in the world.

I would also like to give special thanks to Donnie Vanelli and Dr. Scott Evans for their help and encouragement. Both were in PhD programs in mechanical engineering with emphasis on technology commercialization. Donnie is now the president of a high-technology company in the rapid manufacturing field, and Dr. Evans has completed his PhD and is teaching a cross-listed graduate course in entrepreneurship at the University of Texas at Austin.

Foreword

As a father, I have often wished for an instruction manual for my children. I am sure that many entrepreneurs feel the same way about their new business ventures as they try to navigate the world of decisions that are required for success. Fortunately for both the would-be and experienced leader, this book is a pithy and efficient assembly guide for a business start-up. If only there were such a tool for the challenges of a three-year-old.

My name is Dr. R. Scott Evans. I am working to create technology entrepreneurship and manufacturing programs at the University of Texas at Austin. Within that, I teach a graduate course on technology commercialization that includes students from engineering, the sciences, business, and law. We introduce concepts, theory, and case studies in entrepreneurship to the graduate students. Conceptual frameworks are one thing, but practical details from an experienced entrepreneur are another. Theory does not contain on-the-ground, tactical information.

My friend and mentor, Mr. Bruce Thornton, has written a book on the nuts and bolts of actually starting a business, with advice on where to get the bolts, how much they should cost, and how many people it will take to tighten them. Mr. Thornton has the rare combination of wisdom, wit, propensity to hurry, and preoccupation with cash and survival that is critical to being an effective entrepreneur. Fortunately he also has a penchant for mentoring. More rarely still will you find a person who has the experience of being a CEO for public and private companies for twenty-four years, and who has also founded seven successful companies. He is, at his core, an incurable serial entrepreneur. The good news is that his knowledge and experience has been captured in the pages of this potent book that will encourage and aid other entrepreneurs in their quest for success.

There is a great mystique that has been created around the entrepreneur in our country. Creating value where none existed is certainly worthy of mystique; unfortunately, the popular image of entrepreneurs is built around an incomplete view of the most successful few. We often hear about how much an emergent company sold for, but little about the sacrifices, near-death experiences, and daily decision making that combined to make that moment possible. Worse, it is common to overlook why that company is actually worth something. You may have also read several books and articles that provide rich and brilliantly insightful models for commercialization. Many are very useful, and support the rapid development of a deep conceptual understanding. And, they are incomplete.

"Knowing how a business runs" is not the same thing as "running a business," nor is "the process of starting a company" equivalent to "starting a company." This is a natural and perhaps unavoidable bifurcation between the conceptual, academic incarnation of businesses and their more complex cousins out in the field, in the trenches, or in the real world, depending on your choice of metaphor. The main concepts are vitally important, but when you are in your own venture, your own trial-by-fire school (which I recommend), they only get you so far. Like many rising entrepreneurs, you may be heavily armed with concepts but lightly armored in terms of the details of actually battling your way to a profitable operation. In that case, read on; what you hold in your hands is a field manual for venture success.

Dr. R. Scott Evans

Introduction

I have been accused of being an incurable entrepreneur. My wife and several friends are looking for the cure. I hope they don't find it.

I am a chemical engineer by education turned businessman by necessity, who has started multiple successful businesses in areas such as petrochemicals, horticultural products, technology licensing, organic fertilizers, and rapid prototyping. This makes me a "serial entrepreneur," which almost sounds felonious, but isn't. Some of the companies were sold to public companies, and some are still providing income. The companies normally evolved to the range of $5 million to $40 million in sales, with 25 to 150 employees. My business partner and I look back and remember many good (and some terrifying) times during these start-ups. We made mistakes then and continue to do so during each subsequent venture, but the good news is that most of the time the mistakes were not the same ones, meaning that we actually learned some things. Several of the companies made the founders millionaires, and one of them (Living Earth Technology, now part of Republic Industries) allowed me to retire for the first time at the age of 48. Business development is now my hobby since I don't have to do it for a paycheck. I now enjoy trying to help others learn from my mistakes. One of my attempts to give something back led me to volunteer my time at the University of Texas at Austin and write this book.

This book is a detailed guide to entrepreneurship. I originally wrote it as a guide for graduate (PhD) technologists while I was Entrepreneur-in-Residence and adviser to the Technical Entrepreneurship Society (a role I continue to fill) at the University of Texas. I am also involved in technology licensing and commercialization efforts at the University. I am a director of the Engineering Advisory Council and the chairman of the Commercialization Committee, which has given me insight into commercialization efforts at universities.

The book is written for the entrepreneur who wants to build a company to exploit new technologies or services, and who wants to build a moderately large venture that can go on to the venture capital (VC) or initial public offering (IPO) stage. It will also be helpful to anyone organizing any business start-up, including the person who wants to be successful at the small business level.

This "how to do it with less cash" book will be especially useful for those groups who may not have access to large amounts of start-up capital or those who have not had business management experience. Underrepresented groups in the entrepreneurship world, such as minorities and women (who traditionally have not had access to capital), may find this book particularly helpful.

The book itself is a practical, step-by-step description of the actions needed to organize and run a new venture. It includes detailed advice and examples of state and federal forms, and demystifies payroll and cash operations (bank loans and credit cards). It has sample nondisclosure agreements and advice on how to use them.

It is not "light" reading, and it is not about theory. It is meant to be a reference manual and survival guide for the entrepreneur in a real-world business start-up. In short, it is a practical reference for a successful low-cash start-up, and is best read in stages.

What really happens in business ventures is laid out sequentially in this book—from the idea conception to permanent operations. These sections are about the steps required to build a business while minimizing cash outlays.

This book is certainly not meant as an inspiration for everyone to be an entrepreneur. Indeed, the book may be just as useful if it keeps some people from losing their life savings in a failed venture as it is for those who successfully build a new venture. Those of you who are ready to begin the entrepreneurial adventure are about to risk your savings, your time, and your future. It is important to give yourself every advantage to succeed by developing your company in the shortest time possible to minimize running out of cash, which would usually be fatal to the venture. It also contains a guide to the stages of evolution and provides some of the tenets of management that many successful companies have developed.

I'm confident I will make a case for the critical need to structure your business very carefully in the early days. You will also see many places where I advise getting outside experienced or professional help. The best source of outside help is a retired CEO or business owner who has copious amounts of real-world experience. I often refer to these people as HOGs (helpful old guys). They are an incredible resource and may be the key to your success. The term HOG can apply to helpful men or women, but I will use the term "guys" for convenience.

I have tried to give you some insights into what entrepreneurship is and isn't. You'll also find that it appears that I'm obsessed with cash. The reason is simple: a lack of cash invariably leads to venture failure. I also stress daily operations, because it's the soul of long-term success and profitability.

Before we get into the details of the process, I need to give you my view of entrepreneurship so that the chapter organization makes sense. Let's first take a look at an overview of entrepreneurship and what it really is.

1

Entrepreneurship: What It Really Is

o o o o o o o o o o o o o o o o o o o o o o o o o o o o o o o o o o o o o

Entrepreneurs are serial problem-solvers who search out ineffi-
ciencies and find more practical ways of connecting possible supply with potential demand. In that way they constantly
revolutionize our economy, and have made it possible for average
people today to live longer and healthier lives, with more access
to technology than the kings had in previous generations.

—Johan Norberg

The Italians have a saying, *La dolce far niente*, roughly meaning "the sweetness of
doing nothing." If this is a short-term goal of your life, you might want to stop
reading. To launch a business is a combination of hard work, sleepless nights,
long days, and personal and family sacrifice of time and money. It is a high-risk
time of your life. It's also among the most satisfying and gratifying of times, and a
successful venture is an important contribution to society. Successful new ventures are the major source of job creation and innovation for our country.

WHAT IS AN ENTREPRENEUR?

An entrepreneur is a person who builds and operates a new business. The words *builds*
and *operates* are technically redundant. By my definition, a business is not "built"
until it reaches some stable level of long-term profitability, or self-sufficiency achieved
through efficient daily operations. I say this because there's no magic day that a
business reaches maturity. A business must evolve constantly or it will be outpaced

and overrun by competitors. A few years ago, Robert W. Waterman wrote *The Renewal Factor*. His main message is that successful businesses are constantly renewing themselves to meet the demands of a changing market. He adds that changes are often needed even when business is good. If a business gets "caught out of touch" with the market and behind its competition, then it will suffer.

EVOLUTION OF BUSINESS ANALOGY

The evolution of a business is much like natural biological evolution. Like biological species, those in the business world must actively compete for resources available in the environment if they are to survive. Successful species usually have the ability to rapidly adapt to changing environments and thus accelerate their evolution. Their ability to prosper is directly correlated to being the most efficient in gathering and using resources to generate growth, to reproduce (produce products), and/or their ability to find "food" (cash).

Accelerated evolution also says that you must quickly move through the growth stage, where you are dependent upon others for your food (cash), so that you can find your own sources of sustenance (profits). This accelerated evolution, coupled with small body mass (which requires less "food"), is critical to increasing your survivability chances. What this analogy really says is that small, nimble ventures with few people and a small payroll require less cash to keep going, and can change directions quickly if conditions require it. An early adaptation should be a protective exoskeleton or shell, which we will come to know as a legal incorporation of the venture to protect it from predators.

As in any system, evolution and mutations will naturally occur, and some will work and some will be evolutionary failures. Products that are failures must be quickly recognized and discarded to keep them from squandering resources needed for survivability of the species (larger venture). Mistakes are parasites living off the main body and can cause the venture to become anemic (run low on cash). This weakening leaves the host open to being "eaten" (bought by a competitor) or, as would be the natural progression of weakness, eventual "starvation" (bankruptcy).

The biological analogy is an excellent way to focus on successful evolutionary traits, and should be revisited frequently. So, in business, if mistakes are made, then make them when your business is small and can change direction quickly. You should stay small to limit cash consumption until you "grow up," find a formula for success, and can generate your own positive cash flow. The cash consumption lesson was very visible in the 1990s' dot-com failures. Too often a fledgling organization was expanded too early, and required repeated large cash infusions while the business model was evolving. Often the dot-coms spent cash on items that were ego driven, such as fancy offices and the trimmings. Many never recovered from the debt burden, or from the loss of equity required from venture capital and other outside cash sources.

Evolutionary lesson: Never eat all your food before you know how to obtain more. Thus endeth this initial sermon on starvation (lack of cash) causing an end to further evolution.

HOW DO YOU KNOW IF YOU CAN BE AN ENTREPRENEUR?

I am frequently asked, "How do you know if you can be an entrepreneur, and how do you learn to do everything that is required to be successful?" I have some preliminary comments that I usually offer:

If your experience is narrow and focused, your horizons will need to broaden, primarily by bringing together experts in various disciplines. If you are a master salesperson without any technological know-how, you won't learn about technology by being a better salesperson. Technological geniuses with zero knowledge about marketing can't become marketing experts by enhancing their technological wizardry. Yet, the most critical entrepreneurial requirements—ability to learn quickly and use good judgment—can't be learned in books and classrooms.

My advice is to take a close look at yourself as you read. You need to decide whether striking out on your own is really for you. My thoughts on the type of skills required to start and run a business are discussed in chapter four.

WHAT IS SUCCESS?

Successful entrepreneurship isn't about finding the perfect idea or the "killer application," then sitting back to get rich. It is about successful application of multiple skills to everyday business, and execution of profitable daily operations over long periods.

Also, I do not dwell on the technical aspects of the product or service. This is what the entrepreneur or venture group should know better than I, and scant attention will be given to this subject. I do not intend to diminish the role of new technology or creativity. New technology, especially breakthrough technology, gives you an innate competitive advantage and is very important to increasing chances of success. However a common mistake, especially by technologists, is to assume that most resources will be spent on development. Development of a new product or service is very fulfilling and the most fun. You need to have the self-discipline to do the tedious things, like accounting and bill paying, or the development will never be seen by the public, and the venture will fail.

My hope is that the information presented will keep you from making some of the same mistakes that I have made, and that reading the book will improve your chances of a successful venture. Successful ventures make more efficient use of the world's resources and improve life for all of us, one business at a time.

GOAL OF THE BOOK

One of the goals of this book is to teach you how to start up and organize a venture with minimum cash outlays, so that you can maintain a greater equity position. Another is to show how important it is to put an organization in place early that will work for long-term permanent operations. A business that is in a constant state of reorganization to handle growth cannot focus on customers, markets, development, and cash.

Before we begin the practical aspects of the book, we need to understand what entrepreneurship is and isn't:

- Entrepreneurship, especially technical entrepreneurship, is not about finding a superb idea or the "killer application," and then settling back to get rich off your grand idea. A new technical or scientific breakthrough belongs in a science fair unless you are willing to make the effort to gather all the resources needed to commercialize the idea. It is not glamorous. It is painfully hard work. But it is often financially rewarding and a benefit to society.

- Commercializing an idea requires that you spend about 80 percent of your effort on daily business management skills. This is normally a twelve-hour-per-day grind, alternately punctuated by moments of terror and euphoria. It is dealing with customers (who can be demanding and irritating), bankers (who can also be demanding and irritating), and setting up suppliers and administrative systems to be sure no one is stealing your money.

- Entrepreneurship is enduring frustration with regulations, taxes, and bureaucrats (who can be really irritating). It is about tracking daily cash flow, paying bills, and being terrified that a federal tax deposit may have been forgotten, and the IRS is coming to put you out of business.

- Entrepreneurial activities are good for society, but entrepreneurship is not for everybody. It is not for people who place a premium on security.

- Finally, most of what you see about business on television is purely for entertainment and bears no relationship to reality. Real business is usually not dramatic; it is usually a grinding attention to details, punctuated by very few moments of euphoria (first sale) and terror (I cannot find the money for payroll this week!).

If my vision of the hardships of entrepreneurship has not discouraged you yet, you probably are a good candidate to actually start the venture process. Get some sleep now; you will get less later on.

2

Creating Ideas

I'm often asked, "How do I get an idea for a successful new venture, or come up with a new product or service for which someone will pay money?" I wish it were as easy as taking a special pill, or even entering into a meditative state to boost creativity, but it is not.

SUCCESSFUL INNOVATORS MEET NEEDS

Most ideas come from personal or professional experience. Be alert for products and services you would like to see developed to fill a need in your personal or professional life, and make mental notes to evaluate these ideas as time permits.

Some highly successful innovators have a mental blueprint of their goals. The man who developed the modern helicopter, Igor Sikorsky, had the vision of a science fiction writer. He saw a world where airplanes made of metal transported thousands of people each day at a time when aircraft were covered in fabric and held two passengers. His innovative designs were a fulfillment of his vision.

Other landmark achievements came about to meet a specific need. In the early1960s, the University of Florida athletic department was looking for a way to prevent severe dehydration among its football players. Players were losing twelve to eighteen pounds during a single practice session due to the heat. Dr. Robert Cade, a professor of medicine and physiology, invented Gatorade, which quickly replaces body fluids and electrolytes. Gatorade is the largest selling sports drink in history, and one of the largest licensing revenue sources in the country.

What You Really Like or Hate Can Be an Idea

The lesson here is that if you find something you really like or really need, there is a good chance others like you will like it too. Sam Zell, the New York real estate entrepreneur, lived in the suburbs when he was a boy. On occasion he traveled to the city. On one of his trips he was browsing in a bookstore and came upon a new magazine, *Playboy*. The price was fifty cents. Zell liked *Playboy* and figured, correctly, that his buddies in his neighborhood would share his enthusiasm. For Zell's time and trouble, he marketed his copies for a marked-up price to many satisfied customers. His source for the book supply was his "intellectual property."

The other side of this idea is that if you find something that really irritates you, there is a good chance that it irritates others and that they would pay good money for some method to fix their irritation. For example, trash compactors were invented to reduce daily trips to take the trash to the garage. Then when several days of trash became an odor problem, someone invented a small odor filter for the trash compactor. Pay attention to things that you really like or really hate; many times these can be the foundation of a business idea.

Get Ideas from Universities

For those of you who have business skills but lack technological or creative know-how, universities can be a rich source of ideas. University technical developments and patents are there for the licensing fee, particularly at universities with accessible offices of technology licensing and commercialization. Universities typically generate huge amounts of new technology and patents, but they normally have neither the time nor the resources to commercialize them. Here are some starting points:

- University of Texas at Austin, Office of Technology Commercialization: www.otc.utexas.edu.

- Stanford University, Office of Technology Licensing: www.otl.stanford.edu.

- Massachusetts Institute of Technology (MIT), Technology Licensing Office (as part of their Industrial Liaison Program): ilp-www.mit.edu.

- There are also technology incubators like the Austin Technology Incubator (ATI) and associated Clean Energy Initiative where new technology is in development. See their Web sites and others in your state for more information.

The University of Texas has a policy of aggressively seeking entrepreneurs to commercialize new patents from the university's faculty. UT sponsors two annual events that bring entrepreneurs and ideas together. "Ready to Commercialize" is a showcase of technology that's well attended by angel investors and venture capitalists. The public is also welcome.

UT also sponsors a business contest forum called the "Idea to Product Competition" (www.ideatoproduct.org). It's an international competition of teams, normally made up of one student each from graduate schools of business, engineering, and law, who compete for money and a spot at the Austin Technology Incubator. This contest grades not only the business plan but also the value of the technology and its promise for commercialization. I have been fortunate to judge this competition and thus gain insight into promising new technologies that we may be able to help commercialize as entrepreneurs or investors.

My favorite model of licensing technology is a group of 50-somethings (who have sold their business and are bored with retirement) that negotiate a license on a technology related to their former work. The goal is to find and hire an inventor (often a PhD candidate) of technology. This frees up the businessmen and women to start the business while the PhDs develop the technology. Start-up costs are lowest when retirees forego salaries. The results are good for retirees, the university, graduates, and society.

Conventional wisdom holds that ideas need to be high-tech to be productive. On the contrary, "more-tech" in a low-tech industry can work just as well. In 1985, I joined other investors to start Living Earth Technology, Inc. The idea was based on selling dirt and recycling green waste. Selling dirt doesn't sound like a technical enterprise, but several of our members, including myself, are chemical engineers. By bringing technology to this business arena, we grew to be the largest bulk horticultural products company in Texas. Our marketing plans were based on soil technology, such as particle size, porosity, permeability, micro- and macronutrient (fertilizer) levels, and cation exchange capabilities, of importance to the horticultural industry and the weekend gardener alike. In lay terms, our success was based on bringing a higher level of technology in our products to the market than had previously existed, while educating our customers on why they worked better.

I will use a fictitious company for development examples in the following sections. The company is a composite of several start-ups we have done, including Living Earth Technology. The names will be changed, (to protect the guilty) but the experiences, for the most part, are real. I will call this company "Dirt Technology, LLC" for the duration of the book.

Finding a new idea is important, but it is useless unless you can build and run a profitable business to commercialize it! Chapter three describes how to start preliminary evaluation of your idea.

3

Evaluating New Ideas and Markets

The first step in weighing a new business idea is to screen and evaluate potential market size and probable requirements of customers. Just keep in mind what I call Thornton's Principle of Business Start-ups—something I will repeat throughout this book:

> Entrepreneurship and successful ventures aren't about developing one "killer" application, product, or idea. They're about profitable daily operations that require making hundreds of small decisions, correctly, year in and year out.

MARKET SIZE

With this in mind, a potential market base of five isn't a sound basis for a venture, while a base of several hundred thousand likely is. Be sure to factor in the potential for replacement products or upgrades based on replacing the original ones due to wear or technological obsolescence. In any event, make sure there is enough market to support another supplier (you).

An analysis of markets requires good judgment and intellectual honesty. I have seen many start-ups get into trouble by letting hope triumph over judgment when estimating market size. Often precise data isn't available, especially on innovative ideas. At this point the importance of people (with good and honest judgment), networks, and contacts begins to emerge.

SOURCES OF MARKET INFORMATION

The best source of market information is potential customers. Purchasing agents (PAs) are a logical place to start. Just be sure that the source gives good information, without hidden agendas. Normally, it's in a purchasing agent's interest to encourage another supplier. Even so, try to cross-check information with competing purchasing agents when possible. Various individual and corporate egos can be involved (as well as confidential trade and pricing information), so be very careful how these questions are phrased. Here are the main questions to ask a purchasing agent:

- What is the size of purchases for the current year? And for previous years?

- What are the estimated purchases for next year? Try to get an idea for how fast the market is growing.

- How elastic is the purchase volume on price or quality? Find price vs. volume elasticity. Also find out whether the primary purchasing criteria is price or quality.

- What is it going to take to become a supplier, and what are the criteria for reaching various sales volumes?

- What does the agent like most about current suppliers? What would he or she change, and what products or services will their company need for the future? Find the current supplier's weaknesses to exploit.

- Would the PA be willing to sign a secrecy agreement to allow you to work jointly in order to satisfy those future needs? See if the agent is open to becoming a partner in a stealth program to develop you as a new supplier. If you are successful, you will probably get a contract for part of the volume, and the agent gets another supplier to use as leverage on existing suppliers. You will see more on this in chapter eight under Marketing Strategies.

- Find out the process and timing for qualifying as a new supplier. In some cases it can take a year to qualify and meet all required tests and regulations—don't get surprised here. Be careful: you can burn a lot of cash waiting to be approved.

The tendency of technologists and engineers is to carry out market research on the Web or to use other search techniques. The Web is a good information source, but not for actual market volumes and prices. So, use the Web for surveying competition, and call customers and PAs by phone. Also consider going to retailers who sell competitive products or services and question the store managers. Retailers are a helpful source of historical sales volume information. Always treat retailers with courtesy. Remember to assure them you may be a potential new supplier.

Finally, an excellent source of condensed information is a trade show, where all your future competition and customers may be seen in one location. You should also look for trade publications with advertising while there. Decisions will have to be made about how to advertise depending upon the final consumer. Wholesale customers require a different advertising approach than retail consumers. See how competitors advertise while you do your evaluations.

DECISIONS TO CONTINUE

When considering any potential venture, there comes a time to look closely at data to make some hard, honest decisions about whether or not there is a market for your idea. Think of this as an *evolutionary moment*. Such milestone decisions will need to be made at several junctures during a venture's development. Upon considering the compiled data, does the venture seem viable? Scrapping an idea is painful—I've done this many times—but it's a serious mistake to waste time and money on ideas that have a doubtful future. Answer these questions below honestly, and get unbiased outside opinions where you can:

- Is your product or service unique?
- Is there a large enough market for it?
- Is it likely you can compete with the existing wholesale (not retail) pricing structure?

Assuming you've made the decision to press on with your venture, the next questions to be answered are economic.

EVALUATION OF ECONOMICS

Cost of Production

If you can establish market size and competitive pricing, and can make educated guesses about your ability to capture some of the existing market, you should assess your cost of production. The cost of production should include all raw materials and expenses associated with making your product or service. This includes utilities, wages, salaries, and all other real expenses. The appendix includes a sample profit and loss (P&L) statement that lists typical expenses associated with cost of production.

If you can estimate the number of items to be sold and sale price for the item, you can then estimate your profit. Your first profit potential estimate is your sales revenue minus your costs of production. Profit has different meanings. I use the term **gross profit** to reflect the sales price minus the cost of goods needed to produce the item. **Net profit** is profit after all expenses, as shown in the P&L statement.

Production Feasibility and Economics

After an idea is evolved and you've estimated the volumes that can be sold, the next step is the feasibility and economics of supplying the product or service. This is just one of many times you will need to decide whether or not to rely on your own expertise or engage outside consultants. For example, estimating the design costs of production facilities requires highly skilled professionals in construction and engineering. Production design may sound simple, but it requires years of experience and special training. If you design the organization or facilities yourself, be prepared to double your estimated costs to make up for unexpected or overlooked expenses. The cost of production equipment is the basis for your first **capital budget.** (Look for italicized messages suggesting where special help is needed.)

At this stage, I strongly recommend preparing a preliminary **operating budget** based on your estimated sales volumes and production expenses. An annual operating budget is normally twelve monthly projected P&Ls. An example of items included in an operating budget is shown in the appendix (a typical profit and loss statement).

A separate **organizational expense budget** should also be prepared. The organizational expense budget includes all the costs associated with forming a corporation and other initial start-up expenses.

Predicting these cash needs at this stage is notoriously difficult for the new entrepreneur. All these exercises are really about predicting cash needs, and will give you a realistic basis for your business or strategic plan. My best advice is to get professional help from an accountant, experienced director, or angel investor if available.

Almost all my clients are surprised by the hidden costs of start-up, and by the cost of complying with payroll burden (FICA, Medicare, FUTA, SUTA, workers' compensation insurance, any health benefits, and the cost of reporting and compliance). More information on payroll forms and costs is given in chapter five and the appendix. Underestimating operating costs, capital costs, or size of required staff is easy to do. This will lead to a rapid depletion of cash (cash failure) that will likely prove fatal for the venture. Also, underestimating the time required to get a business up and running is the norm. Delays cost money and should be planned for. A good rule is to expect that it will take twice as long to get a project going as you think it will. Have enough money to withstand these delays.

An excellent method for checking or estimating production economics is to engage an outside toll processor. A toll processor is a manufacturer who will custom manufacture items for a fee or give you a bid to do your production for you. A toll supplier normally will have an existing operation and experience in operations, and can give you an excellent reality check.

Note: Be sure to sign a nondisclosure agreement (NDA), as shown in the appendix, before discussing your product with the toll processor!

Now comes the big question: How much profit is needed to move ahead with the venture? The answer is quite a bit, because the estimated profit always seems to go down as reality sets in and you get more details. A better gauge is whether your product or service has a fundamental competitive advantage, either better technology, enhanced performance capabilities, or production or materials breakthroughs that will allow you to be the low-cost producer.

Evolutionary moment: After developing preliminary sales volumes and production economics, it is time to decide if you have any competitive advantage over existing suppliers or products. Can you really compete and make a profit? If so, proceed to get organized as shown in chapter four.

CASE STUDY: DIRT TECHNOLOGY, LLC

Dirt Technology evolved from discussions about by-product streams in the petrochemical industry. Dudley and I started looking for analogies for large underdeveloped streams of materials that could possibly be upgraded, and we saw thousands of tons of grass being sent to the landfill every year. We also were both avid gardeners and vegetable growers. We evolved to the point of thinking about getting paid to take grass and green waste, grinding and composting it, and selling the final product to other gardeners to enrich their soil. We particularly liked the idea of getting paid to take it, and then getting paid again when we sold it.

We first had to prove that we could make a useful product and make enough money to have a business.

A quick survey of disposal fees at local landfills and sales prices of topsoil and potting soil indicated we had enough margin to cover some manufacturing costs and that there was a large market for the products. We believed that being paid to take the raw materials would give us a fundamental competitive advantage in the market. Initial manufacturing estimates and market surveys (we called other suppliers for prices) were also positive. We felt that the overall market for bulk soil and mulch materials in our area was probably $30 million/yr., and our original estimates showed we could break even at sales of about $500,000/yr. At 20 percent of the market ($6 million in gross sales), we thought we could make $1–1.5 million a year in net profit before income taxes.

We were thrilled. We made the decision to proceed to initial organization activities. We had very little idea of what hurdles lay in front of us. Chapter four will take the reader back to the organizational details, and we will find out more about Dirt Technology.

Note: The basis for the 20 percent of market is that a comparable or better product should be able to grab that much market share from people who either are looking for something new or dislike the current supplier. This is a judgment and market feedback estimate, and probably requires the help of a HOG (helpful old guy retired from a related business).

4

Initial Organization Procedures

○ ○

An empowered organization is one in which individuals have the knowledge, skill, desire, and opportunity to personally succeed in a way that leads to collective organizational success.

—Stephen R. Covey

It is also one that does not run out of cash!

—Bruce C. Thornton

Creating an organization that covers the main operating functions is a necessary step toward ensuring the success of your company. The immediate goals involve developing human resources and satisfying a company's legal requirements under the law. The following steps are critical:

- Finding key people with critically needed skills
- Developing a strategic plan
- Choosing a company name
- Developing a legal structure (and registering with the state and federal governments)
- Analyzing types of legal structures
- Creating the legal structure or corporation
- Creating and submitting articles of incorporation to the state, and getting a state charter
- Purchasing a corporate record book and seal

- Obtaining a Federal Employer Identification Number (EIN)

- Creating stockholders' agreements and other legal protections

- Protecting intellectual property and trade secrets

- Developing accounting and administrative systems

The initial organization includes determining the critical resources needed (primarily people) and the type of legal form of your company.

FINDING KEY PEOPLE WITH CRITICALLY NEEDED SKILLS

There is a fundamental trade-off between maximizing your share of the equity in the company and using that equity to attract and keep critical people to ensure success. The prudent course is to decide what skills you need, and use equity to obtain those skills instead of paying high initial salaries. Maximizing the number of good people with diverse skills is like buying insurance for success. Minimizing the size of initial payroll will guard against cash failure. At the end of this chapter, there's an example of the amount of equity used to obtain skills and critical functions in Dirt Technology. This discussion should give insights to my thoughts on appropriate negotiated-equity levels.

Finding good people is probably the hardest part of entrepreneurship and requires more subjective judgment than any other activity. Networking skill or finding a HOG is very important. Here's a list of critical skills that are normally required for a company start-up:

- Management

- Marketing/sales

- Financial/accounting

- Product or technology development

- Production

- Strategic planning

All of these skill sets should be held by people who can learn and evolve quickly, and who can perform in more than one area. Please see chapter ten for some management tenets by which to judge prospective managers.

Management

Management is about coordinating the other positions. Effective managers see a broad perspective and have the ability to see the "forest." They need to guide the evolution of the business by motivating and working with others. Management is also about planning—ensuring that employees get the right resources and information to do their job. Ensuring the right resources at the right time requires an ability to anticipate future needs and to visualize the future. I have included a section on management tenets that will help the new manager be effective (in chapter ten).

Marketing/sales

Marketing is the development of sales and product strategy, the determination of which markets to pursue, and how best to position the product. Sales is the maintenance and execution of the marketing strategy.

Financial/accounting

Normally, the financial/accounting function oversees all cash activities and the systems that account for transactions, including bookkeeping, tax strategy, bank operations, cash management, and information technology (IT) work. Note that there is a difference between developing numbers for accounting purposes and management information purposes. Accounting is a tightly regulated method of "accounting" for cash and taxes. Management information can be obtained from accounting numbers, but it is usually in the form of customized reports that allow decisions to be made or operating efficiencies to be compared.

Product or technology development

Product development is another term for research and development, and should include technical evaluations of competitors' products.

Production

Normally, the head of production is responsible for most of the people and spending in the organization, and will consequently have the most headaches. The marketing people will usually get some of the glory that this person deserves, since the marketing groups are associated with sales and income, and production is associated with costs. Everybody loves income and hates costs.

Strategic planning

Strategic planning involves determining the company's direction and deciding where and how to compete (and sometimes *if* you can compete). Rather than place this job in the hands of one person, I prefer that this be carried out by the leadership team (the positions listed above) at regular meetings.

Very rarely will you find all these skills in one person, but on occasion you will find someone possessing two or three. Again, attract promising individuals for your team through your promise of equity, rather than higher salary, to cut initial cash outlays. The only skill that you might think about outsourcing initially is accounting/payroll, however the bookkeeping function should not be out-sourced. You must keep control of cash and check writing, and cash levels should be reviewed daily.

I am frequently asked how to find good people and how to decide whether a person meets the "good" standard. My primary rule is to either hire people I know or take advice on them from someone I trust. In other words, it's a matter of networking.

My standard for who is "good" is based on my assessment of four attributes of an individual:

- Are they experienced?

- Are they highly intelligent?

- Do they display good judgment?

- Are they intellectually and personally honest?

Technical abilities can usually be measured or taught. It is very difficult to teach honesty and good judgment. These characteristics are among the most critical to the success of your venture. Remember, these people will be making decisions and spending your money when you're away.

At this point you should have found and decided upon key people, and negotiated equity positions. Once your leadership positions are filled, it's time to set up a company that will give you and your people some liability protection. This means some form of corporation, limited liability company, or limited liability partnership. Do not start any operations without this legal protection! This will be your protective "shell" to keep others from "eating" your personal assets.

You should now proceed to developing a strategic plan and a corporate or legal structure. You should also introduce the ideas of shareholder agreements, noncompetition agreements, and issues below to the key people now, and have consensus on these issues while you work on your legal structure. Find out now if you have any serious internal disagreements in the team about strategy, management style, or direction. Disagreements that surface later can be very detrimental to the venture's survival.

DEVELOPING A STRATEGIC PLAN

The first step is a joint meeting of your key people. Experience shows that they should spend at least one full day away from all distractions to decide on a business model. This includes an organization structure, a plan to make your products, and a plan to market and sell the products. You also have to recognize the realistic limits of what can be accomplished, based on your resources of experience, manpower, cash, and time. The purpose of the plan is to formally organize your thoughts, products, and plans for the business. Finding a HOG to help bring experience and reality to these discussions is very helpful. Also note that many people use "strategic plan" and "business plan" interchangeably.

A good strategic plan has the following elements:

- Description of major product(s)

- A review of the market, its size, and your initial marketing strategy

- A review of key people and experience. Do you have the right people to develop and run a successful business?

- Description of resources and people needed to produce the product and to implement permanent operations.

- A decision whether to be a manufacturer or to use a toll manufacturer. Initially you may want to be a development company and license your developments, or even be a franchiser. A decision not to be a manufacturer may limit the overall size of your business, but it has the advantage of minimizing cash requirements.

- A chronological plan describing your stages of development and growth, with a projected time frame to move from initial organization to profitable long-term operations.

- Estimated cash requirements at each stage of the plan. This should include planned responses to running low on cash. Is everyone prepared to go without pay? For how long? Do you have backup plans to bring in outside money for dilution of your equity? These questions will almost surely arise.

- A review of competition

- Analysis of fundamental competitive advantages compared to competition. Do you think you can survive if existing competition tries to keep you from entering this market? What happens to your profitability if competition cuts prices in response to your market entry? How much can you cut prices and survive?

- A summary of long-term goals. Though this is not necessary, it is helpful to summarize the overall plan. Listing long-term goals may also reveal whether all key people have the same vision for the company or its exit strategies. Incompatibility should be found early.

- Visions and values are not goals, but standards of operation that will guide the decisions of the company. Values such as honesty and integrity are not window dressing; they need to be followed religiously all the time.

Your strategic plan should be kept confidential and up-to-date. You must have this plan before you can move to initial operations and before you can prepare meaningful marketing strategies and initial budgets. This is an excellent exercise in discipline, combining strategic thinking with realistic limitations. There is no substitute for experience and judgment here. I strongly recommend that you find someone who has built or run a business to help you. The soundness of your strategy, and your ability to present it, may be the key to obtaining outside cash, so do not hurry through this process. Remember, you should update this plan frequently as you evolve.

Note: Do not think that your plan is all about presenting and developing your technological innovation or "killer app." Your plan is about convincing yourself and others that you can build and operate a successful, profitable company. Your biggest challenge will be finding cash and, once found, managing it. Spend a lot of time discussing cash: where it will come from, how to minimize costs, and what you are prepared to do when you run out of it. If you have to go to venture capital people, get professional help in negotiations.

Evolutionary moment: You should now have preliminary estimates of market size and profit potential. From this point onward you will start to spend significant amounts of money. Stop now if you have any major doubts or large disagreements within the team.

Choosing a Company Name

Once you and your team have picked the best corporate structure, there are ways to create the entity without spending a lot of money if you are willing to do some of the work yourself. After you decide on the best structure, you have to decide on a name for the venture to use for legal registration. The name should be both descriptive of what you do and evocative of good images.

I have clients who make common errors in naming, particularly in technological areas. A name that does not describe your business function is confusing for purchasing agents and can make marketing efforts more difficult, especially for passive sales efforts like Web-based information. If the business name does not indicate a principle function of your venture, potential new or non-technical customers may pass it over in favor of a business that appears to meet their needs by name alone. Placing such a self-inflicted impediment on your marketing efforts is very poor business, especially when it could so easily be avoided. It is hard enough to fight competitors without handing them customers.

At the primary level, a name should be descriptive of what you do or produce. At the secondary level, it should evoke images that you want to project. This can be accomplished by using such words as "technology" or "advanced," words that leave good subliminal impressions. Finally, the name should be easy to pronounce and spell; otherwise you will spend a lot of time correcting people and will risk muddying your company's image. Seeking outside consulting from a public relations and communications firm is helpful when you tackle a creative decision. There are public relations firms that work almost exclusively with technology-based companies and understand how best to translate complicated and technical issues so they are comprehensible to consumers.

Next, it is time to build a protective exoskeleton or corporate shell to protect you as you venture into the world.

Developing a Legal Structure

The goal of this section is to show how to get a corporate charter registered with the state so that the new entity can begin business with some legal protections. The following organization forms should be discussed with your legal advisor and your critical people as an outgrowth of your business plan. A summary of advantages/disadvantages of each form is given below.

Analyzing types of legal structures

C Corporation. This entity provides personal liability protection for the stockholders, directors, and officers under most circumstances. Protection from personal liability generally means that you cannot be held liable for debts or bankruptcy of the venture. The C Corporation is very flexible in the number and types of stockholders. The primary disadvantage is that it is subject to double taxation. That is, corporate profits are taxed, and any after-tax profits distributed to stockholders are taxed again as dividends. There can also be double taxation of the profit from selling your company. This is a complex issue and will not be covered here since I do not recommend this structure for start-ups.

Sub-S Corporation. This entity provides personal liability protection like the C Corporation, but without the double taxation problem. All profits of the Sub-S Corporation are taxed one time as income of each shareholder, and the pro-rated profits are reported on each shareholder's personal income tax form. This type of corporation has some restrictions on shareholder type and nationality. An election to become a Sub-S corporation should be made at the time of organization. A conversion to a C Corp can be made under the proper circumstances. You must file an IRS form 2553 Sub-S election by March 15 of the year following incorporation to get the tax advantages.

Limited Liability Company (LLC). This organization functions almost like the Sub-S Corporation and has the same tax advantages. It has some different restrictions on types of shareholders.

Limited Liability Partnership (LLP). This type of entity is really for professional organizations like legal firms or doctors' associations, and will not be discussed further here.

I believe that the Sub-S or LLC organization form is the preferred vehicle for most start-ups, but again, seek professional legal and tax planning advice.

There is an excellent discussion on choosing the best structure for your business in an article by a friend of mine, Michael C. Riddle, a Houston attorney. The article is titled "Choice of Business Entity in Texas" and was published in a copyrighted edition of the *Houston Business and Tax Law Journal* (volume 4, 2004). The discussion is applicable to other states as well.

Note: As you learn more about accounting, you will discover that the primary goal of a privately owned company is cash flow maximization first and profitability second. Picking the right legal structure will maximize cash and minimize reportable profit, and will retain cash by lowering taxes. There will be more explanation of this strategy in chapter five.

Creating the legal structure or corporation
Find out if your chosen name is available

Once the name is picked, it is time to call your secretary of state to see if your pick is still available. The secretary of state maintains all corporate records, and you start building your corporation here. In Texas, this is one of the more competent and least-bureaucratic government organizations with which I have ever dealt. Note that the type of legal structure has to be picked before the exact name can be chosen, since the name must include "Inc." or "LLC."

The Web site for the Texas Secretary of State's office is: www.sos.state.tx.us. For other states, visit the state government Web site. You can also call and ask them to do a name search. If your chosen name is available, you can get them to reserve your name while you do paperwork, or you can pay an additional fee to hold your name or expedite your application for registration.

Creating and submitting articles of incorporation for the state

The goal here is to get your articles of incorporation registered with the state so that the state can issue a corporate charter. You can then conduct business under the protection of the charter, and can open bank accounts and enter into legal agreements as a company. You will first need to choose a legal registered agent. This can be you or your attorney. (Having an outside law firm serve as corporate agent is a prudent action, as they will have a more permanent address and will understand the ramifications of legal correspondence, and the fee is minimal.) You will then fill out the forms with the name of the agent and the legal address, and name the organizing officers and directors of the corporation. (Note that an LLC has members instead of stockholders and has a board of managers instead of a board of directors. Do not let this confuse any issues.) All state legal documents will be sent to this address, and anyone wanting to contact you for legal or compliance issues will be able to find this information at the secretary of state's office.

You will need to write up articles of incorporation (it's easy to find examples in the self-help legal books or on the secretary of state Web site) or pay a lawyer to do this. I have also included simple examples in the appendix, and the state Web site has a generic form you can use.

Note: Some attorneys charge as much as $5000 to set up a new corporation. By following the preceding directions, you can do the same thing for yourself for about $400.

You should send a check to the state with the articles (articles of incorporation for a Sub-S and articles of organization for an LLC), and the secretary of state (www.sos.state.tx.us) will issue a charter and charter number to you, making it legal to do business in the state. This charter can be revoked if proper payment of state franchise tax or corporate state tax is not filed, leading to the owners becoming personally liable for any operations or activities done after revocation. This is called loss of protection of the corporate veil. For all issues of franchise and sales tax in Texas, the Web site for the state comptroller is www.cpa.state.tx.us.

Another useful site in Texas is www.edinfo.state.tx.us. This is a good site for general business information and has a directory of available assistance for starting and operating a business.

Purchasing a corporate record book and seal

The most cost-effective way to get your corporate seal and record book is to call a lawyer's service company and order your corporate book. It will come complete with all the forms, including the Sub-S election forms, blank stock certificates with your name, and a corporate document seal. The total cost of this book starts at about $60. (In Texas, I have found Liberty Legal to be a reliable source for this record book. Call 800-392-3720, or visit their Web site at www.tcs-libertylegal.com for more information.) You can also pay an attorney to do this.

Keep your state, federal, and corporate documents in a secure but accessible place. You will be asked for copies of many of these documents to open bank accounts and apply for loans. Most banks require a copy of the charter, the articles of incorporation, and a corporate resolution to open a checking account (a typical resolution form is in your records book).

Note: If you have used personal checks or funds to get started, now is the time to complete expense reports and reimburse any personal funds spent on corporate or venture business. This will ensure that the full protection of your corporate veil is not jeopardized by intermingling personal and corporate funds.

Obtaining a Employer Identification Number or EIN

You next need to use a form SS-4 (available on the IRS Web site: www.irs.gov) to apply to the IRS for an Employer Identification Number (EIN). This number serves the same income tax purpose for a corporation that a Social Security Number does for an individual. It is also used for payroll tax reporting.

You should now be a new legal entity in the eyes of the state and federal governments. You can begin legal operations as soon as the state returns the approved charter and articles of incorporation and you have opened a bank account with the state required minimum amount of assets (money). In Texas you must have $1000 or its equivalent before you are legally allowed to start business operations.

Being a corporation has some other requirements to stay legal, such as having officer elections, reporting changes in officers to the state, and having regular board or stockholders' meetings. Failure to keep your corporate records up-to-date can lead to increased personal liability for the owners (penetration of corporate veil), a potentially fatal error. (See chapter eleven for more on this subject.)

CREATING SHAREHOLDER AGREEMENTS AND OTHER LEGAL PROTECTIONS

It is always exciting to actually issue stock certificates in your own company and sign as president or secretary on the certificates. However, before you do any of that, you should put more legal protections in place, which consist of the following:

- **Shareholder agreements:** Agreements among the principle organizing shareholders that cover goals, salary strategies, cash and dividend policies, potential exit strategies, and restrictions on the sale of stock.

- **Noncompetition agreements on principals, officers or shareholders**

- **Confidentiality agreements**

- **Non-poaching agreements**

- **Assignment of ownership rights** to any technology, proprietary market information, or economics developed prior to formation of the corporation.

Note: None of these agreements should be finalized without proper legal help and oversight; the issues are too complex, too subject to change, and too important to do otherwise.

Shareholder agreements

Shareholder agreements are really good insurance that your critical people have considered—and are in agreement about—future plans for the company. The agreement could be considered a type of conflict resolution guide for any future disagreements as well. In the event of the death or divorce of a shareholder, the agreement also offers protection from the spouse or other relatives who may have a different agenda. For this reason, I recommend that all spouses sign the shareholder agreement.

Shareholder agreements may cover such diverse subjects as:

- Officer salary ranges
- Stock options policy
- Stock sale restrictions
- Obligation to sell stock back to company in the event of death, divorce, or disability
- Stock valuation methods for buyback or resale
- Agreement on exit strategy
- Any other points of potential conflict among large shareholders
- Conditions, procedures, and obligations for future cash infusions

Legal advice from an experienced attorney should be sought when deciding what issues the agreement will address. I recommend that the principals write the agreement themselves in plain English, and then have it translated into a legal document. Doing the first draft yourself is a good exercise, and it cuts down on iterations and revisions.

Noncompetition agreements

I recommend that a noncompetition agreement be executed with all principals, officers, and shareholders. This keeps key people from starting a competing business if they should resign or be fired from your team. Though difficult to enforce legally at lower employment levels, such agreements usually have moral and psychological force. This is an evolving section of employment law, but my interpretation of the law in many states is that the agreement is difficult to enforce unless you can show specific compensation tied directly to the agreement. In other words there must be separate consideration for the agreement, and having to sign a noncompete just to be offered a job will not be enough. Having such a document will usually help protect you from someone leaving, taking your plan, and starting the same business in your geographical area. Get expert legal counsel here; this legal area is complex and changes rapidly.

Confidentiality agreements

I recommend that all employees sign a confidentiality agreement to protect technology, business trade secrets, customer lists, internal economics (both cost and sales information), and sources of supply. These agreements put employees on notice that they cannot use such information against you if they leave and can actually make current employees more aware of confidentiality breaches. Loss of trade information can seriously hurt your ability to compete or make adequate profit. Please see the appendix for an example of a confidentiality or nondisclosure agreement (NDA).

Get legal help here.

Non-poaching agreements

These agreements can also be used for all employees, but are difficult to enforce. Basically these restrict the ability of any ex-employee to raid your organization for experienced employees to work at a competing business or start-up.

These have some moral and psychological impact, and have more legal impact when more than one employee is approached to leave.

Get legal help here.

Assignment of ownership rights of development work and patents

1. All pre-corporate development work should be formally transferred to the new corporation. This is an easily overlooked item and can be very costly or destructive if disputes arise among the principals.

2. All employees should sign an assignment of invention and patent agreement, to make sure all know that the corporation is paying them to develop new ideas that are the property of the company. The employee rights to inventions are given up in consideration of getting a paycheck.

Now that you have gone through the intellectual exercise of developing all the agreements, you can actually issue stock certificates and collect money. Be sure that you collect enough money to satisfy state minimums. For example, you are not legal in Texas unless you collect more than $1000 in cash or goods. Next, you should put your accounting procedures in place to protect your intellectual property (IP) and to manage your cash.

PROTECTING INTELLECTUAL PROPERTY AND TRADE SECRETS

As you develop your business and business plans, you may develop ideas that can be protected with patents. As we just saw, these ideas and patents should be covered by invention agreements or assignment agreements.

If at any time an idea or invention needs formal patent protection, then the process of acquiring such should be initiated. Note that obtaining a patent is expensive and can take two to three years. Expert legal help is a necessity. Advice on when and how to file, and especially any need to file in foreign countries, should only be considered with this legal help. Patent costs can reach $10,000 in the United States alone, and can reach two to five times that amount if many foreign countries are included.

A decision must be made whether to patent an invention or practice, or whether this disclosure gives too much information to the market and your competitors, who may be much larger than you. Protecting practices or trade information with rigorous secrecy may sometimes provide cheaper protection. How you choose to proceed may depend upon your business model, and whether you are a technology licensor or whether you can be a great execution company. A technology licensor will almost always have to have patent protection to collect licensing fees. On the other hand, a company with the ability to execute quickly and protect sources and procedures may want to try to outrun the competition without any formal disclosure of inventions or practices. This last option keeps others from learning what you know and trying to circumvent or break your patents. Protecting against patent infringement can be extremely expensive and can put you out of business.

Note: Intellectual property protection is a very specialized legal area, with many "gray" areas. Get qualified legal help here early and be prepared for some substantial legal bills.

DEVELOPING ACCOUNTING AND ADMINISTRATIVE SYSTEMS

Now that you have a bank account and cash from initial stock placement, it is time to set up accounting systems. It is essential to the management of your business to set up your cash management system with the proper software. It is much more efficient to run all transactions (checking, invoicing, accounts payable, accounts receivable, and possibly payroll) through an entry-level system (Quick-Books, Peachtree Complete Accounting, or the equivalent). You can do much of the system setup and daily entry yourself. Try to run all transactions through the system so that all reporting is complete and does not need to be hand-adjusted. This is especially necessary for payroll. If all transactions, including payroll, are run through the system, a daily P&L can be run from standard reports included in the software. Daily, complete reports are a valuable tool to manage your business (and especially cash). The systems mentioned above are quite powerful and will cost less than $500 for multiuser licenses.

Your accounting system will provide the basis for all accounting and reporting. It will also provide management information (this is different from accounting information), which is the most important information you have about the daily status of your business.

Note: Your business will most likely succeed or fail based on the information in this system, so give it your highest priority!

If you are not familiar with accounting terms or procedures, get help! I suggest taking a short course on accounting fundamentals. You have no business (no pun intended) starting a venture without basic understanding of income (profit and loss) statements and balance sheets. You must have some knowledge of cash flow procedures and basic taxation before you can begin to optimize your cash flow and profitability. If you do not have these skills personally, add someone with these skills to your team. You must have this expertise in the venture on a daily basis.

You should now have your key people, a business plan, shareholder and other agreements, an EIN, and a legal charter before proceeding. You will also need a state unemployment tax account number within one quarter of paying salaries or wages. Contact your state employment entity to get signed up. The Texas Workforce Commission Web site is listed in the appendix.

Note: It pays to take time to organize carefully and to organize for the long term. Many potential problems and conflicts can be avoided by picking partners for their expertise, compatibility, and common ethics and goals. Much time can be saved from having to continually upgrade accounting and management systems by doing it right the first time. You will need every minute of that time to run the business during the next phase. You do not want to be distracted by bouncing checks, payroll mistakes and the IRS, or lost credit with suppliers!

CASE STUDY: HOW DIRT TECHNOLOGY FARED IN ITS INITIAL ORGANIZATION

We started our operation in my living room. We continued development of our business model, which was to charge a fee for greenwaste coming in and to sell compost product going out. We knew a complete manufacturing and delivery organization would be required to do this.

Our first decision was an excellent one, and that is that we would start our initial operations while we were still fully employed in the petrochemical industry, and still had paychecks. We were very careful not to shortchange our existing employer. It would have been unethical to work on our new business during business hours at our "day job."

We next assessed our skills inventory: Dudley had marketing and purchasing covered; I had manufacturing, finance, and organizational management covered; and Dudley and I both had creative technical skills and strategic thinking abilities. We needed sales and accounting help, as well as daily operational continuity while we were still at other jobs. We had some confidence in this assessment, since Dudley was a senior vice president of marketing, and I was president of our chemical company, which had sales of about $40 million at the time.

We asked a good friend, Mark, (CPA and MS in computer science) to be our accounting and tax guru, and found Richard, who had excellent horticultural credentials, to be our sales expert. Finally we found Peter, who was an oilfield operations supervisor with excellent mechanical skills and operations experience. We made him our initial operations superintendent while the rest of us held down our other jobs. Peter was young, but he was very intelligent and experienced for the age of twenty-four. He was also inexpensive for the operational expertise that he brought to the team.

We allowed Mark to buy 4 percent of the stock, and asked that he provide accounting oversight and monthly financials for "free" for the privilege of ownership. He would also set up initial accounting software and control procedures. He was a company controller and head of systems in his day job, so this went smoothly (thanks again, Mark!).

We allowed Richard to buy 10 percent of the stock, and agreed upon a starting salary when we got to that point. After his day job, he was to gather market information.

Peter had no initial capital, and we made an arrangement for "sweat" equity, that is he would receive 2 percent equity in exchange for each of the first two years of service if he were still employed by us at the end of those years.

Dudley and I set out to make some initial product in our backyard by buying a four-horsepower chipper/grinder, grinding up our own grass and leaves, and making a compost pile. Our wives loved this (not!). This was a failure all the way around: a compost pile has to be about eight feet tall to decompose rapidly, and our grinder and backyards were not capable of this.

Our strategy evolved over a popular brand of beer, where we decided to approach a local landfill to see if we could convince them to divert all greenwaste entering the landfill, and stockpile it for later operations. We subsequently traded 5 percent of the equity to the landfill operator for access to five acres to start operations. As part of the agreement with the landfill operator, he diverted all his greenwaste to us for "free." Note that we were originally capitalized for $25,000, so we did everything we could to minimize cash outlay, including trading equity for an operating site. We also wanted the landfill operator to have a vested interest in our profitability and success.

The decision to become a Sub-S corporation was Mark's, based on the expectation of operating losses in the first year or two (tax planning). Mark set up our initial accounting software and payroll systems, and we became a legal entity with the federal and state governments.

We wrote stockholders' agreements that restricted sale of any stock to outsiders, and on the advice of attorneys, we had all spouses sign all agreements. We actually followed the procedures in this chapter closely.

Our first organizational problem appeared here. Since Peter was not a U.S. citizen, we found that we had to quickly reorganize as an LLC to allow his ownership. This reorganization cost more than all the other legal work put together.

Note: Do your homework here to avoid these costs.

We found a used construction trailer, put it on our section of the landfill site, and put up a sign. We were ready to start initial operations. Richard was pushing us to make some semicommercial quantities of compost for samples. We had one employee, one trailer, one computer, a phone number, and a plan. It was time to turn on the lights and make something.

Note: Actually getting the electricity and initial phone number set up are difficult when you are brand new and have no credit history. Be prepared for deposits, personal guarantees, delays, and hassles. The first real troubles developed as we tried to make some production samples for our sales efforts. We will see more after chapter five.

5

Initial Operations

Initial operations include developing a marketing strategy and producing prototypes while holding the line on spending. I find that it is difficult to consider producing prototypes without having some market feedback on concepts. There is an element of "chicken or egg" here. You need to have a product or service to discuss with potential customers. On the other hand, you want to avoid revealing something that either doesn't meet their needs or would leave a poor impression that could be lasting.

This is the time to complete your efforts to find a customer "partner" as mentioned in the development section. The marketing effort needs to get into high gear at this point, and you need to accelerate the evolutionary iterations between the customer and your development group. Remember, you are "burning" cash while this work is in progress. Please consult chapter eight for additional marketing help.

EVOLVING A PRODUCT

Concurrently you must start developing your production methods and costs, and evolving them as you get customer feedback on suggested changes to your product. You should be building your budgets and economic models with the feedback from your marketing and development groups. Your marketing efforts, your product development, and your venture economics should be evolving concurrently and interactively.

This will be repeated many times:

Customer evaluation ➡️ **Product modification**

⬆️ ⬇️

Revised prototype ⬅️ **Revised cost**

Note: This is one of those times to revisit the biological evolution analogy. Think about evolution and adaptation abilities here.

At some point your potential customer will want a prototype to evaluate, which means you are actually going to have to produce something.

PROTOTYPE PRODUCTION

A prototype is a preliminary working product or service that a potential customer can evaluate, under real-world, commercial conditions. It should be obvious that a successful product is the cornerstone of a successful venture. Likewise, nothing is more damaging to your credibility than a prototype that doesn't work or that fails under real-world conditions. My advice is to be patient; adequate research and testing guards against your showing an immature product.

A primary concern here is how to produce a working product while keeping capital and production costs to a minimum. Do not spend money on production or even semicommercial production facilities while rapid product evolution is taking place. This is where the computer that is built in your garage or the service that can be simulated and programmed at night is important. There is a trade-off between spending a great deal of money on product development (which takes up cash that may be needed for more iterations or survival), and producing a garage-built device that is cheap and allows for many revisions, but may not look as sleek or have as many bells and whistles on it. This requires knowledge of your customer and, ultimately, good judgment. There is also no substitute for preparing your customer for the level of development of your prototype before you present it.

For more sophisticated or expensive devices, the possibility of toll processing should be evaluated. Toll processing is when you pay someone else who has flexible processing facilities to produce a commercial product to your specifications and design. It is an excellent way to produce a commercial product without the full cost of building production facilities. For a simplified example, building a chip production facility can easily cost upward of a billion dollars, and you would not want to risk this kind of money on a newly designed, unproven development chip. With the proper confidentiality and noncompetition documents, you might be able to find a producer to make a trial run for you, with a moderate capital cost for special modifications. You also should define your needs for production data logging, both to understand how to design your own facilities and to quantify costs.

Finally, many purchasing agents and companies will not sign purchasing contracts without having a commercially produced product(s) to use in their commercial production facilities. In many cases, banks and VC groups will not loan or invest money without a signed customer contract. This often leads to the Catch-22 situation of needing the loan to build the facilities to produce the commercial demonstration product, but you can't get the loan until you have a product to get the sales contract. This can be a real problem for the entrepreneur, and toll processing (with good intellectual property and trade secret protection!) is my best answer for this problem.

News flash! There are dishonest and unethical people in the world. Use NDAs anytime you deal with outsiders, especially when production methods or raw material suppliers have to be divulged.

PREPARING A BUDGET

You should now have better information on your venture, and based on that information, you should attempt to update your operating and capital budgets.

Capital Budget

A capital budget is the amount of money spent for fixed or depreciable assets like equipment and buildings. It is easy to say "design and then estimate the cost of your required production facilities." But the reality is that this very challenging, and usually technical, exercise is outside the scope of this book. Get outside help here from experienced production or construction sources.

It is very easy to underestimate not only the amount of time involved, but also the cost of start-up and production facilities. Out of hundreds of capital projects I have observed in twenty years, only two have come in under budget. Most of these projects were undertaken by professionals at Fortune 500 companies, with a great deal of staff oversight and experience, and 99 percent of them overran their budgets. This should serve as a warning for the new entrepreneur. If you are sleeping well as an entrepreneur, you are either exhausted or missing something.

One of the purposes of this budget is to determine the net capital that will be required, so that the proper interest and depreciation costs are available for the operating budget. You will need to know these amounts to do a cash flow projection from the combined capital and operating budgets. Usually money can be borrowed from banks to partially finance items in the capital budget, and that borrowed money will affect the cash required from other sources. Get professional help from someone with operational experience, like an angel investor, senior director, or a retired executive.

Note on budgets: Optimism is essential to entrepreneurship but optimism often leads to cash failure when a budget is involved. Learn to be a pessimist when you produce any budget.

Operating Budget

The operating budget is your best estimate of sales revenues and costs for a given period (usually twelve monthly periods). This budget should include your estimated sales revenue and every expense you expect to incur. The "bottom line" of this budget shows your expected profit for the period.

Usually this budget is broken down into administrative expenses, also known as SG&A (sales, general, and administrative) expenses, which tend to be relatively fixed or independent of amount of product made and sold. The other part is the variable expense portion, which tends to vary based on the number of units manufactured and sold.

Items such as actual salaries and wages, raw material costs, insurance, telephone service, interest, and depreciation all go into this budget. Some of the expense items like phone bills, are actual expense and cash outlays; some, like depreciation or other accruals, are expenses in the long run, but are not actual cash outlays.

Preparing the operating budget is an excellent exercise in intellect and self-discipline (a typical profit and loss statement and budget comparison can be found in the appendix). It makes you think in detailed terms about what is really required to run your business. I would never think of trying to operate a business without this exercise. It also provides a good basis for incentive and bonus plans. Without a good budget, it will be difficult to attract new capital. Indeed, much of the evaluation of your management abilities is based on the realism in your budget projections. A product of the operating budget is an estimate of cash flow, which is discussed below.

Caution: If you base bonuses on how much the budget profit is exceeded, there is a tendency for managers to minimize the budgeted profit to increase their bonus. Conversely, you do not want to set a budget that is too far out of reach, or everyone will feel it is unattainable, and as a consequence, will limit his or her output. Bonus plans are discussed in greater detail in chapter nine.

CASH FLOW

I've been accused of being obsessed with cash flow. You'll join me when it's clear that cash flow is the do-or-die equation of a venture. Detailed explanation of the differences between profit and cash flow is the subject of an accounting course and is beyond the scope of this book. However, let me explain some basic concepts that the entrepreneur should know.

First, you always want to strive for positive cash flow, and you can have this sometimes even when your budget and income statement show a loss. You can also have negative cash flow sometimes when you show a profit. This sounds counterintuitive, but here is how this works:

Your income statement (P&L) and operating budget assume steady-state operation (no changes in inventory levels or working funds, etc.), and includes non-cash items like depreciation and other accruals. There is a sample P&L in the appendix for you to review to help understand this concept.

Depreciation is a charge you take to your income to reflect equipment wearing out. You don't write a check each month for this effect, but you will have to replace the worn-out equipment some years in the future. This is a method of showing the expense of using up your equipment (monthly expense) whereas the actual lump-sum purchase of the equipment might be done once every five to seven years. The IRS will not let you write the entire purchase price off at time of purchase, so you have to expense it in increments according to an IRS formula. Therefore you reflect "consumption" of an asset by showing a monthly expense, but no cash is actually paid out based upon depreciation.

There are also cash effects from non-steady-state operations, as when your inventory is increasing or when sales and your accounts receivable (A/Rs) from sales are increasing. Changes in inventory or accounts receivable are examples of cash effects that do not affect profit or the P&L. How does this work?

For example, let's say you buy twice as much raw material in one month as is necessary for that month's production. Generally accepted accounting procedures say you can expense the raw material used in the product, but only for products you actually sold in the month. The rest of the raw material goes into inventory and is shown as an asset. You are able to expense part of the raw material on the P&L, but you have to write a check to the supplier for all of it. The increase in inventory does not hit the P&L, but you still have to pay the cash out. Similarly, if you sell one hundred widgets, you can book the sales revenue for the P&L, but your customers may not pay you for as long as ninety days. You made the sale, but will not actually get the cash for forty-five to ninety days. So the P&L shows a profit, but you actually lost cash for a short period of time. Many companies that are profitable on paper run into cash problems, especially companies that are growing quickly and have rapidly increasing inventory and accounts receivable.

Note: In the early days, cash flow is more important than profitability. This is explained in greater detail in chapter eleven.

Evolutionary moment: After the customer feedback, prototype evaluations, and development of realistic operating economics, do you really have a product that can compete and be manufactured and sold at a profit? Can you find enough cash to start operations, buy inventory, and pay some salaries? If so, move on to commercial operations.

CASE STUDY: DIRT TECHNOLOGY CONTINUES

When we left Dirt Technology, we had failed to make any useable compost in our backyards, and Richard was pushing us for some commercial samples for initial sales efforts.

A board meeting produced a plan to buy a commercial chipper to make some commercial-sized compost piles for some realistic samples to evaluate. At this meeting we put together a capital budget and operating budget. The capital budget included a front-end loader to "turn" or mix the compost piles; we were surprised by how far we underestimated the pricing of a decent used machine. Reality struck a harsh blow at our bank account. What we actually had to spend for equipment was about twice our capital budget, and the extra down payment affected our cash position and left us with little operating funds. Dudley and I made personal loans to the company to make payroll for Peter and Richard.

It was good that Dudley and I still had our day jobs.

At this point we took some brush and grass from the landfill and began to grind it with our new chipper. We invited the banker who financed the chipper out to the site to show off our expertise. We had ground up small limbs before, so Peter decided to show the extremes of our capabilities and managed to put an entire 8-inch-diameter tree into the chipper feed system. The chipper responded with the mechanical equivalent of a hernia, blowing a hydraulic hose and spraying hydraulic oil all over the banker. We survived the dry cleaning bills, but still cringe at the memory of this disaster.

Lesson: Never do anything for the first time in front of customers or bankers.

We went on to fix our chipper, and several months later we made small quantities of commercially produced compost. For our next adventure, we brought the president of a large nursery out to see our wonderful product. His evaluation was that it was wonderful compost, full of humus and fungus, but that no customer would buy it for mulch, since it would continue to grow fungus. It did not matter that it was beneficial fungus; the customer would absolutely not buy it for cosmetic reasons. We had a technical success and a marketing failure.

In light of what appeared to be a failed business plan, Dudley and I started calculating how much money we could salvage if we shut the venture down. We also did some technical work to see how to stop fungus using organic methods, and discovered that tree bark has natural antifungal properties. We were successful in testing and making compost-bark blends that were excellent products. We went on to become buyers of bark from lumber operations. Next, research determined how much bark and compost to blend to have a good technical and cosmetically salable product. We survived by making a 90-degree turn in our business plan while we were small and nimble. We adapted, evolved, and survived.

Lesson (especially for technologists and engineers): You can have a product that is technically a success, yet fails once it reaches the commercial market. Do not whine about the injustice and lack of technical appreciation of the customers; just fix the problem, or go out of business.

Note: We never did sell any product to the president of that nursery. He never forgot the poor product we showed him and the poor initial impression we made. This was another painful lesson learned.

No one said that evolution would be painless.

We were soon able to get some commitments to buy our blended products. We next had to ask ourselves whether we thought we could ultimately make any money, and if so, whether we would have enough cash to survive until we were profitable. We needed a production facility and efficient production process. This is easy to say and spell, but not to do. We all quit our day jobs and went to work full time trying to set up permanent operations. Dudley and I each took a 60 percent cut in pay to have this fun.

6

Commercial and Permanent Operations

This phase is concerned with operating the venture to produce a product at a profit. The critical issues are management related rather than developmental. If you still want to work in development, then have professional managers in place who understand that their job is successful execution of operations. This includes marketing, manufacturing, quality control, and management and motivation of employees.

Commercial/permanent operations will require much larger amounts of cash from the sources listed in chapter seven, and will require expertise in financial and administrative control. It may also include project and organizational management responsibilities. At this point we're not just dealing with venture development, but rather business operations management directed by strategic planning. Optimizing management of an operating business is a subject for separate study. Please see chapter ten for some related comments on successful management of operations.

I would like to reemphasize the thought about entrepreneurship and operations one more time to start this chapter: Entrepreneurship and successful ventures aren't about developing one "killer" application, product, or idea. They're about profitable daily operations that require making hundreds of small decisions, correctly, year in and year out. They are about not running out of money so you can stay in business!

The administrative procedures that you need for successful daily operations are usually too mundane and unglamorous for MBA classes, but we are going to discuss them for your benefit. We will talk about:

Operations related to sales and billing

- Invoice language

- Credit procedures
- Accounts receivable and collections
- Credit card functions
- Sales tax

Paying bills

- Approval
- Cash control
- Check writing

Human resources

- Payroll
- Benefits
- Taxes and governmental requirements
- Workers' compensation insurance

OPERATIONS RELATED TO SALES AND BILLING

Sometimes selling something is easy compared to actually getting paid for it. We will talk about procedures to protect your rights to get paid, and how to go about collecting money. As you get bigger and more professional, you will sell things on credit, with a promise from your customers to pay you within a set period, normally thirty days.

Invoice Language

Though most people will never read your invoice, it should contain terms and conditions of payment and rights you have if the customer fails to pay on time. Liability limitations are usually included, as well as an explanation of your rights to recover attorney's fees if you have to sue for collection. An experienced attorney should review your invoice for this important, but often overlooked part of your invoice.

Credit Procedures

Before you sell to anyone on credit, you need to have them submit a credit application along with references, so you can see if they are credit worthy, are sales tax exempt, etc. Your credit application should include the following:

- Request for sales tax exemption certificate: If you don't collect sales tax, and the customer should be paying it (but is not), you may have to pay it! More on sales taxes later. Keep good records here. You will probably be audited in your first five years.

- Request for personal guarantee: If your customer is relatively new or has a poor credit history, then you should require a personal guarantee. This means that one of the officers of the customer's company agrees to personally pay the invoice if his company does not. Judgment is required here. You should not try to force a company like IBM to sign a personal guarantee, but you will probably want a fledgling dot-com that has been in business for two weeks to sign.

- Request for references: Get credit and trade references (corporate credit cards are good too). These references will not help if you don't actually call them. Ask about payment history and the maximum amount of purchases in a monthly period.

Keep a file of completed credit applications (with original signatures) and sales tax certificates. You should decide on and assign a credit limit and put this limit in your accounting system.

Accounts Receivable and Collections

As you get larger and begin to sell products or services on credit, you need a system to keep track of who owes money and how old the promise to pay is (called accounts receivable, or A/R, aging). All previously mentioned accounting systems will keep track of invoicing, payments, and resulting lists of who still owes you money.

Most large companies are taking about forty-five days to pay bills that are due within thirty days of date of sale. Some very large companies will tell you in advance that they will not pay you for ninety days, and that is the price of doing business with them. This is an example of the golden rule: "He who has the gold makes the rules."

If, after sixty days, payment has not been received, you should start to worry that there might be a problem. Your chances of getting paid rapidly decline after that date, so act quickly to recover your losses!

One of the ugliest jobs in a company is having to badger people to collect overdue A/Rs. The person charged with carrying out this task will hear every excuse for not being paid, and will get lied to and abused daily. My preference is to have the salesperson that sold the product call the person who bought it and apply pressure. Simple issues can usually be sorted out by your accounting people talking to their accounting people, but complex or large problems should be solved by the salespeople. After all, they are the ones who wanted to sell to this customer, and they need to get feedback on who is not paying and why. Judgment is required here to decide whether to continue to sell to the company or person in arrears. I don't recommend cutting the person off; instead, put them on COD for future orders until the old debts are paid.

Note: In my experience, if you refuse to sell to a customer in arrears until they pay up, they will just take their business to a competitor—and you will increase your chances of never being paid.

Credit Cards

Payment of bills is progressing toward credit card and other electronic procedures and away from payment by cash or check. Most people have never thought about what actually must occur for money to be transferred by electronic means. Today there are bank services that sell or lease the modems required to verify creditworthiness and to actually record the credit card transaction. This requires phone lines and paying a service fee to the credit card company. The service fee is usually between 1.5 and 3 percent, with the premium cards like American Express being at the high end. This cost can be a significant part of your profit margin and should be budgeted. The good news is that the risk of nonpayment then transfers to the credit card company. Talk to your bank about getting started with credit card operations.

Sales Tax

Most states require collection of sales tax on final sales of goods or services. You should apply for a sales tax number from the state after you become a legal corporation and receive your federal EIN.

In most states, you must collect sales tax unless you have a reseller's or other exemption certificate from your customer. If you sell to final users, you must collect taxes, file monthly reports, and send collections to the state. If you do not collect the required tax and your customer does not pay the tax, then you are usually liable for paying it. Protect your venture by keeping proper sales tax certificates on file for all customers. Collecting the proper amount of sales tax can be difficult due to various taxing authorities taxing different sections of metropolitan areas. Many times there is a state portion, a city portion, and a mass transit or other county portion. Collection of each depends upon where you and your customer are actually located. A state comptroller's office can give you guidance here.

Consult your accounting professional for rules on collecting and paying sales taxes, and making monthly sales tax deposits. See the appendix for a sample of forms required.

PAYING BILLS

Paying bills is also known as accounts payable operations. This is a major part of cash handling and control. Proper administrative procedures are necessary to guard against theft or embezzlement and to maximize cash retention. I recommend the following steps:

- Each invoice received for goods or services should be approved by the person who ordered the goods or services (I like initials).

- This approved invoice should then go to a different person, usually a senior executive for his or her approval and a date to pay (initials and a date). The doubly approved invoice should then go to bookkeeping for entry into the accounting software.

- On the indicated date, a check should be printed, attached to the invoice, and submitted to a senior executive in charge of cash control to sign and release the check, or to hold if there are problems. All the latest accounting software packages have cash projection features that show existing cash levels and projected cash requirements for bills coming due. Good cash control and projection is vital to staying in business. Even smaller companies should use double-initial controls for paying invoices.

Note: Never let the same person approve the bill, print the check, and sign it. Get at least two people involved to make fraud less likely.

HUMAN RESOURCES

A venture's greatest asset is its people. A venture's most troublesome problems involve personnel, also called human resources. An organization's human resources department is normally responsible for the following items:

- Payroll
- Benefits
- Taxes and governmental requirements
- Workers' compensation insurance

Payroll

Payroll can be handled with outside groups such as ADP, Paychex, or Century Payroll Services (a division of Century Business Services, CBZ). Because of the need to transfer money to outside services, and the need to transfer data back and forth, I favor doing payroll in-house on your own software. It is essential to morale, and to sound business ethics, to keep payroll records confidential. The software programs mentioned earlier have the ability to restrict access to payroll information by using passwords. Use these protections!

Benefits

Benefits vary with the age and size of the company. Retirement plans and health benefits are often a nightmare for a start-up, so get expert help from a financial or benefit adviser like Century Business Services or AXA Advisors, LLC.

Taxes and Governmental Requirements

Payroll tax withholding and deposits are another potential nightmare. The accounting software programs do a good job of keeping track of these liabilities, but setting them up initially requires some skill or professional help.

There is no one place you can turn to for all the rules and regulations, so I will try to summarize the various taxes and reports you face:

The primary taxes everyone knows about are federal withholding (from the employee), and Social Security and Medicare (from both the employee and company). The money that is withheld for all three must be deposited in a bank account using form 8109-B (Federal Tax Deposit Coupon), or can now be done electronically. These are called 941 tax deposits and a quarterly 941 summary form must be submitted. The tax deposits themselves must be made at various frequencies (every week to every quarter, depending on payroll size). You can also pay all these taxes online with the federal EFTPS (Electronic Federal Tax Payment System). You can enroll or make inquiries at 1-800-555-4477.

Also, federal unemployment tax (FUTA) must also be submitted to a bank at regular intervals. The state unemployment taxes (SUTA) must be submitted to the appropriate agency in your state (in Texas it is the Texas Workforce Commission). The federal and state amounts are interactive and complicated, with the federal tax being paid on the first $7000 of each employee's wages or salary and the state taxes on the first $9000 (in Texas) for SUTA. The state rate is based on experience and updated each year, and the federal rate is based on whether you pay state unemployment, so the rates are interactive. This is not a joke. *Get professional help here.*

Most states require quarterly employment statements and payments. The federal unemployment tax deposits are known as 940 deposits, and a form 940 is used for transmitting federal unemployment money.

Once a year all of the federal wage and withholding must be summarized and sent to both the employee and the federal government in the form of W-2 statements and W-3 transmittals. Also, many states and cities have income or franchise taxes on corporations. Most states require annual status reports on the corporation, as well as sales tax reports and franchise annual tax reports. Neglecting these filings and payments will normally be fatal to your venture. Please see the appendix for some examples of governmental forms. Get accounting help here unless you have had payroll experience.

Note: Some people try to escape this paperwork by having "contract" workers, who are responsible for their own payroll taxes. This can be dangerous, especially if the contract workers are really your employees in the eyes of the IRS. In this case, if the contract worker does not pay employment taxes, then you are liable for them in most cases. Get legal advice here if you are considering this.

After reading the above, who wants to replace the IRS with a national sales tax? Most current business owners do, and most entrepreneurs will. Knowledge is power, but sometimes it is not fun. For help with filings, see both the appendix and the following Web sites: (Texas) www.twc.state.tx.us/customers/bemp/bempsub3.html, (California) www.taxes.ca.gov/forms1.html, or see the equivalent site in your state.

There are other governmental requirements, both state and federal. An example is OSHA, a federal agency that requires that a form relating to reportable injuries be posted. You can be fined for not posting this notice or making the injury report available. There are other notices that must be posted, from sales tax certificates to employee rights required by state agencies. See the Web site above or the appendix and the list of useful Web sites for state help sites for forms for new companies.

Workers' Compensation Insurance

This is a special type of disability and accidental death insurance that I highly recommend. This insurance has statutory limits on how much an injured employee can receive for injuries incurred on the job. The liability limits are fixed. Without this insurance, a venture can be open to unlimited lawsuits for injuries to, or death of, an employee, both for actual injuries and for punitive damages awarded for negligence. Lack of maintaining this insurance can be a fatal error for an unlucky venture.

Note: All of the above information on administrative procedures is sometimes enough to persuade an entrepreneur that the start-up is not worth the struggle. The difficulties of starting a new venture will be easier to bear if you enter the process with some understanding of the costs and frustrations you will encounter.

CASE STUDY: DIRT TECHNOLOGY STARTS COMMERCIAL OPERATIONS, SUCKS CASH!

Dirt Technology set up the administrative systems mentioned above, with some evolution through mistakes and successes. Some painful lessons were still being learned.

Lesson number one was about cash flow. Since we were new, we could not get credit from suppliers and vendors, or if we did, it was limited. This meant that we had to pay cash for equipment repair, and for outside trucking and raw materials. On the other hand, we had to issue credit to large established wholesale customers to take them away from competitors. The larger we got, the more cash was being consumed for inventory buildup and increased accounts receivable. After year one we started showing some profitability, but we were losing cash to these "working funds." We proudly showed our positive monthly profit and loss statements to our spouses and told them that we were doing so well that we only had to loan another $10,000 to the company this week. This "success" was a hard concept to sell at home.

We finally were able to get a loan from the bank based on inventory and A/Rs. Profitability finally turned into positive cash flow. By the time we obtained our loan, we had loaned the company ten times as much as our original stock capitalization. This made us obsessive about cash conservation in all future ventures.

Lesson number two was that no good deed goes unpunished. We set up health insurance for employees after we grew to ten employees (we eventually had over one hundred), but our health insurance company went bankrupt. We would have been covered through a state pool, except our last check to the insurance company had been posted a day late, and by law, the state statutory pool did not cover us. The same day one of our salespeople was diagnosed with cancer. We ended up having to post a letter of credit with the treating hospital, and we paid all bills out of cash flow. The bills were massive, and we almost had to declare bankruptcy, but we were able to negotiate the hospital bills down by paying cash, and we survived. The obsession with cash was growing.

Lesson: Cash failure can arrive from an unexpected direction, even during permanent operations, when you think you should be past these types of surprises. Keep a source of backup cash available to help ensure success for the venture.

We had many other strange and unglamorous events happen to us, from dealing with one of our trucks that backed over a septic tank and partially fell into it, to suffering stolen computers. We had hard decisions to make, such as whether to drop products that we liked, but that the market didn't. (Another hard decision was deciding which one of us was going to go work with the commercial wrecker to get our truck out of the septic tank). We evolved and had the discipline to shed the things that did not allow us to grow. We had always had a goal of selling out to a public company, and we sold "Dirt Technology" to Republic Industries (now Republic Services Group—NYSE) in 1990. How did we do? At the peak value of Republic Industries, our company stock would have been worth about $40 million. We certainly did not get this maximum value, but it shows the reader the scale of what is possible, even in "normal" times.

Exit strategies are a subject for another book. However, I will give you a way to keep score on the potential value of a venture. We did acquisitions for Republic Industries and others, and we found that we could offer to buy a company for about five times the pretax profits of that company, using public company stock as the currency. So remember to keep those expenses and salaries low, since every dollar of expense takes about five dollars out of the value of the venture at sale time.

Note: I want to add a personal note of thanks here to two well-known entrepreneurs, Michael G. DeGroote and Wayne Huizenga, both whom I met at Republic. Mike was also the founder of Laidlaw, and Wayne was the founder of Waste Management, and together they did Blockbuster Video, Republic Industries, AutoNation, Century Business Services, and others. To my knowledge, as president or chairman of Republic Industries, neither took a salary from the company. They both had options and warrants worth millions, but their interests were completely the same as the smallest stockholder, and their lack of taking a salary kept us from depleting badly needed cash in the early days. This was a valuable lesson for me and should be for other CEOs who take large salaries and bonuses while their companies lose money and stock value. Mike, you are still my hero! Thanks for all you did for us.

7

Funding: Early Sources of Financing and Cash

Cash is the life source of any venture. Because it's highly unusual for a new venture to generate cash from operations in the first year, the focus in this chapter is on outside sources.

Early sources of cash include the following forms of equity and borrowing:

- Equity or paid in capital for stock ownership—from savings, friends, or outside investors

- Loans

- Other cash sources

EQUITY

Equity financing (cash) is the result of sales of ownership (stock) in the company. The amount of cash may be based on the perceived value of the future company or the projected initial cash needs. Each state has rules (see secretary of state Web sites) stating the minimum capitalization (total money paid into the treasury for stock) required before operations can legally begin. Decisions regarding the level of initial capitalization will be discussed below.

Personal Savings

Obviously, you and the other principals want to supply much of the equity financing so that you can maximize your ownership percentage in the venture. The first source is your savings account, but here's a cautionary note when deciding how much to use.

- You may lose all of the initial equity, since entrepreneurship is very risky by nature.

- You should reserve some savings for future equity calls*, or emergency funds needed to keep the company alive. A new venture almost always has additional capitalization needs, and if you cannot meet your share of the next capital call, then your ownership is diluted.

- You may have to pay for food and rent out of savings if the venture cannot pay salaries to owners during cash shortages.

An equity call, or cash call, is a request for all shareholders to put more money into the treasury on a pro rata stock ownership basis. Any stockholder that is not able to meet the call will have their ownership position reduced.

Friends and Family

Many times the first round of equity is offered to friends and family, and they become stockholders. I find that it is easier to make difficult decisions when friends and family are not stockholders, and I personally try never to get family involved. I would save this source for emergency loans in a cash crisis. However, if you involve friends and family, they should be required to sign all stockholders' agreements, and they should be given full disclosure of risks and responsibilities for future equity calls. The disclosure needs to be done by a lawyer.

Outside Investors: Angel or Venture Capital Equity

If the principal owners cannot supply enough equity cash to take the company to the point of cash breakeven, and banks or others will not loan money, then sale of equity to outside investors must be considered. The two major sources of outside equity financing are angel investors and venture capitalists.

In reality, neither of these two sources may be interested in providing equity cash at the first level of start-up. Both tend to be cautious, and the terms for providing cash are severe. There is a very good comparison of the recent state of angel and VC financing in a paper from Stanford University, titled "Note on Angel Financing."[1] This is a good starting point for anyone considering outside equity financing. The crash of the emerging markets with attendant VC losses has

---

1.   "Note on Angel Investing," Alexander Tauber and Grousbeck, Stanford University GSB, March 1998.

convinced many VC and angel investors that the time of funding the "killer app" is over. The day of requiring a company to have a competent management group for business operations is here. The ability to execute is now the key to success.

In this climate, all outside financing sources will require a business plan (basically a strategic plan that you should have done in the initial operations), annual operating and capital budgets, and a good presentation to make them feel that initial management is up to the task of developing and managing the venture. This may be the first major test of marketing skills for the venture. If the entrepreneur has to use outside sources for financing, he or she may be facing dilution of ownership to minority status and restrictions on management decision-making.

I favor using an angel investor first, because the terms are usually a little better. You can also get valuable experienced management help, particularly when the angel investor has experience in your business area. The angel investor's contacts and experience are often the key to whether the venture survives. Also, many angel investors are not only looking for a good investment, but something to occupy their time; or perhaps they are getting involved to give something back. This is why they usually contribute more free time than VC groups. How much equity should founders expect to keep if angel or VC money is required? This is a complex issue, but generally the answer depends on the level of development of the business operation. A new entrepreneur who can actually entice angels to invest will probably receive 10 percent or less of the equity, if 100 percent of the funding is from the angels.

LOANS

Remember, **the primary reason for new venture failure is lack of cash or cash (flow) failure,** so spend quality time on protecting your cash position. Get loans when you are in good financial shape, because chances are that you cannot get financing when you are already in trouble. Be creative, and do not be afraid to ask for better terms, conditions, or extended terms. As my business partner Mr. Warner says, "All they can do is say no, and every once in a while they say yes."

Loans come in many shapes and sizes. Remember any loan must be paid back with interest.

Bank loans

There is an old saying that banks only want to loan you money when you have enough money that you don't need to borrow it. Unfortunately, this is partially true.

Banks are usually very conservative and want all loans to be covered by collateral and personal guarantees. They are reluctant to loan money until operations have commenced, so this is not a source for start-up financing.

Having said all that, banks can be a source of operational funds, from signature, working line, and equipment loans.

Signature loans

These are loans that do not have defined collateral. They are based on personal assets of the person seeking the loan. Interest rates are based on the asset base of the person seeking a loan.

Working lines

These are loans based on a percentage of qualified accounts receivable or inventory. Banks will normally loan from 50 to 70 percent of the amount of inventory (at cost) or 60 to 80 percent of qualified accounts receivable, (usually A/Rs less than sixty days old, or those that are considered "current"). This type of loan is critical after operations start and growth rate is high. These loans replace badly needed cash as sales increase, and the company has paid for increasing inventory levels, but has not yet been paid for product or services sold. Interest rates are usually 1 to 3 percent over prime, either floating on the prime rate or at a fixed interest rate for one or more years. Begin discussions on these as soon as initial operations begin.

Equipment loans

Both banks and equipment makers make loans collateralized by the equipment. Banks will require a down payment, usually at least 10 percent, and will require personal and corporate guarantees. Interest rates are normally floating at 2 to 4 percent over prime or at a fixed rate for the life of the loan. Note that many states will exempt equipment purchases used in manufacturing from state sales tax. Get professional accounting help in your state on this issue.

Loans from sellers

Often the terms and conditions of loans from equipment and property sellers are better, especially from motivated sellers. Equipment sellers will often have incentive financing or "no-down-payment" (other than sales tax) type financing, which can minimize cash outlays. These loans will be collateralized by the property or equipment you are buying and can sometimes be obtained without personal guarantees.

Interest rates vary from 0 percent incentive rates to fixed loan rates in the 4 percent over prime level.

Lease instead of buy

Many times equipment manufacturers or property owners will consider leasing instead of selling. This is especially important in real estate or office needs and with some large equipment. Some equipment makers offer a capitalized lease, where you essentially own the equipment at the end of the lease, but the seller gets depreciation tax credits. Get professional help in evaluating these options, since they may have tax consequences. The advantage of leasing is that it normally allows minimum initial cash outlays.

SBA loans

Another source of pseudo-public financing is Small Business Administration (SBA) loans. (SBA) loans are a source of start-up money for some small businesses, but come with typical governmental strings and restrictions. SBA loans are loans made from banks, but with federal loan guarantees that reduce the interest rates. You can investigate these types of loans and requirements at www.sba.gov.

OTHER CASH SOURCES

Extended terms from suppliers and vendors

Often raw material suppliers will be open to extended terms for a new customer, but this must be negotiated with some consideration for the extended terms. Sometimes you can agree to a slightly higher price for materials in exchange for those terms. This in effect becomes a short-term loan, where you can sell the finished product or service and get paid for it before the bill for the raw material is due. Other times vendors will agree to delay payment, especially in times of recession or highly competitive markets. The term for this is increasing the "float" and is a good no-interest type of short-term loan.

Prepaid sales to customers

Rarely will conditions arise where customers are willing to advance payment for future delivery of products or services. Some consideration is usually needed for this, such as reduced prices, price increase protection, or guaranteed volumes. This can essentially act as a no- or low-interest short-term loan, and is a good way to increase cash availability.

SBIR and other grants

Grants are available for technical innovation and research from federal and state programs and the National Science Foundation, among others. Some come with "strings," but the SBIR grants are sizeable and fairly clean. SBIR stands for Small Business Innovation Research grants, and is run out of the Small Business Administration federal program. Again please see www.sba.gov.

Tax and regulatory incentives

As of this writing, the U.S. Senate along with a group known as the National Commission on Entrepreneurship plan to recommend a package of tax and regulatory incentives to promote entrepreneurship. There is no guarantee that anything useful will come of this, but you should remind your professional accountant to stay abreast of any tax or regulatory breaks available from this work.

Minimizing federal taxes to conserve cash

There are many legal methods to minimize cash payments for federal taxes. The need here is to maximize non-cash deductions to reduce taxable profit. Taking deductions should not affect your cash flow, but should lower your income tax payments. Typical methods include maximizing depreciation, taking research and development (R&D) special credits, and setting reserves for questionable A/R accounts. Accruals and depreciation require professional accounting help, but be aware that these approaches are useful and possible.

8

Marketing Strategies, Pricing, and Sales

This section gives you some of my favorite strategies to penetrate new markets, and the best development strategies based on an analysis of your competitive strengths. Remember, marketing is about determining your customer's needs and explaining why you or your product can best fill these needs. Marketing is not sales. Marketing is about strategy. Sales is about executing that strategy and maintaining customers.

Entry-level marketing is difficult, because you are small, and your competition is normally larger and well established. Many species of small animals have a survival strategy of being difficult to see. This also works in the business world.

In this section we will discuss how to use small size as a competitive advantage, and ways to minimize the disadvantages of being an untested supplier.

We will discuss the following strategies:

- Stealth partnership (with market leader)
- Smaller company, more responsive
- Technical prowess
- Aura of quality
- Low-cost producer
- Formulator plan or "bundling"

MARKETING STRATEGIES

Stealth Partnership (with Market Leader)

Note: The stealth partnership is my preferred entry marketing strategy, and has been very effective every time we could find a partner.

Classical economics teaches that it is difficult to enter a new market. The existing suppliers will have advantages of economies of scale, which will allow lower pricing. Also, one of the usual responses to a new competitor is for the existing supplier to cut prices to keep customers and market share. An effective way to bring a new product to market without disrupting the current pricing structure is to secretly partner with a customer. The best candidate is either the market leader or the fastest growing customer. Here is what you propose to the customer:

You expect to enter the market with a superior product and want a customer to work with you in the final stages of development. In turn you will give the partner customer-preferred treatment. For example, your company will sell to the partner at a lower price for a specified period in exchange for an estimated annual volume sales contract. The contract will allow your company to have a defined sales volume to begin the business. Please consider these additional benefits of such an arrangement:

- The new venture gets actual commercial feedback on the product under development, under conditions where the customer does not initially expect it to be perfect. The customer expects to work through early failures or problems.

- The new venture does not face the rejection of an initial shipment, which is very damaging to reputation and image of the venture.

- The customer gets to design the final product to fit its exact needs and is psychologically committed to the product, since the customer helped develop it.

- If it truly is a breakthrough product, then the customer gets an advanced look, and you have time to jointly evolve the customer's product in secrecy to get a jump on competitors.

- As an intangible benefit, your company works closely with a market leader. This allows your company to learn about the customer's future needs, the overall market, the competing suppliers, and often the customer's competition (potential other customers for the venture).

- Most of the time, personal relationships are developed that are invaluable for future business.

At some point the relationship of your company as a supplier to the stealth customer will be known in the marketplace. This creates instant credibility with other customers. This usually expedites sales of your products to the other customers, providing, of course, your agreement with the stealth partner allows you to sell to others. This can be a very tricky legal area, so make sure to get legal advice.

My preference is to give a price concession to the stealth partner, with this customer's full knowledge that you will sell to competitors at a higher price. Giving a price discount to the stealth partner for the consideration of helping develop the product and for contracting an estimated volume is legal, but must be done correctly. Get legal advice or help from an HOG here.

I also like to use "meet or release" provisions in my stealth (and other) contracts. A meet or release clause says that the customer agrees to a set or formula price, but if a competitor of yours offers the same product at a lower price (with the same terms, volumes, and conditions), then the customer can demand that your new venture either meet the price, or release the customer to buy some or all the product at the lower price from your competitor. The new venture has the final decision as to whether to match the price or let the sale go, which is still a good position.

This is a reasonable compromise to get a high-volume contract without making the customer take high risks. From the customer viewpoint, becoming contractually dependent on a new, unproven supplier is highly risky, and there have to be incentives and consideration commensurate with the risk for them to sign.

It is very important to find a customer with integrity and honesty with whom to work through this stealth process. Also, the proper legal protections (such as confidentiality agreements) and a letter of intent written in non-lawyer language must be in place, so that the expectations of all parties are understood. A typical confidentiality agreement is shown in the appendix. Please consult an attorney before using any legal document to be sure that any unusual circumstances are covered.

Smaller Company, More Responsive Strategy

This strategy can be very effective if your company works with a customer with a high evolution rate. This type of customer will value a very responsive supplier with short cycle times. This is an excellent way to differentiate your venture from the larger, slower reacting, already established suppliers, and is a good way for a small venture to gain entry.

You will almost certainly have to find a contact within the customer's organization that is either in operations or has intimate knowledge of the use of the product. It is difficult to use this strategy while working solely through the purchasing group. This strategy can also be used by larger ventures as a marketing differentiation. It is important to listen to the buyer or customer to see if this resonates or is a priority with the customer. This is a very effective strategy to turn what could be considered a weakness (small size) into a strategic competitive advantage. It is a good marketing method for a new venture trying to enter into a new market.

Technical Prowess Strategy

If the venture has a product or service that "runs faster and jumps higher," then this is a useful strategy. The only way to know if your venture has technical advantages is extensive knowledge of the competition and marketplace requirements. Be careful here that you do not have a technical success, but a commercial failure (do not use this where nobody cares that your product runs faster or jumps higher, except you). What's more, the technical prowess strategy works only if you are dealing with someone who understands technical advantages and how they can be used. Caution: Explaining technical advantages to a non-technical manager or purchasing agent will frequently result in this information being lost before it gets to a decision maker.

Communicating with and through the technical departments will allow you to find out what technical advantages may flow through to the ultimate customers of the client. This information can be used in marketing discussions. Engineers in technical roles are also likely to discuss sensitive commercial information that a manager or purchasing agent would never divulge. Be careful with this; your engineers could also be naïve about divulging your commercial information to others, making this a dangerous two-way flow. This is a good reason to educate everyone in your company about sensitive commercial issues and how damaging leaks can be to the new venture and its employees. It never hurts to frequently remind your employees that their paychecks are dependent upon the success of your venture!

Aura of Quality

A frequently used differentiation is the "aura of quality" theme. Basically this strategy attempts to show that the product from the new venture has quality advantages over the competition, and that these quality issues can increase sales or have quality advantages for the customer. Often this strategy can result in higher pricing and higher profit margins, or can be used as a way to persuade a customer to try the new venture's product. Another point is that a company's reputation for quality can enhance other product lines by association. Note that quality can mean either reduced defects or an enhanced product.

Low-Cost Producer

One of the most basic marketing strategies is to supply an equal or better product at a lower price. Most customers assume that a new venture is a higher risk supplier, so there has to be some incentive for the customer to try the venture. Lower pricing is a very basic motivator. However, once this tactic has been employed by the new venture as an inducement to try the product, it becomes difficult to quickly raise prices. It is a great competitive advantage and sales incentive to be able to continue offering low prices, but it means that the venture must be the low-cost producer to stay in business. Let me say once more that operating efficiency and excellence in execution should be top priority for the new venture, in this case to allow it to be the low-cost producer.

This strategy is particularly useful in economic downturns, when customers are more interested in cutting costs, or when the customer is looking to increase market share. Also, if this position can be achieved, it will then insulate the venture from being the weakest supplier in the field and the first to fail in a recession. Being the low-cost producer allows price-cutting to gain market share, or price maintenance to keep profitability up to build cash reserves.

Too often, new ventures, and even mature companies, are lax about being the low-cost producer in a field until difficult economic conditions force them to think about efficiency. This human weakness can be fatal to a venture in downturns.

Note: It is sometimes easier to start a venture and be the low-cost producer during an economic downturn. In a downturn, most existing companies will resist downsizing, even as sales decline and costs do not. For this reason, most existing companies will find it difficult to lower prices when they see a new competitor entering the market. Existing companies usually will become high-cost producers, as they resist cutting jobs and instituting layoffs. It is human nature to procrastinate when faced with unpleasant duties, and this can be used to the advantage of the new venture.

Formulator Plan or "Bundling"

We first saw the "formulator" plan when competing with a major chemical company, and we were so impressed that we added it to our permanent list of marketing strategies. This plan really works better for the market leader that has multiple products. It is very difficult to compete with this strategy as a new venture. A simplified example of this plan works like this:

Company A has four products that it sells as a related product line. Company A has a pricing structure that gives a 10 percent price discount to all customers who regularly purchase all of their needs from Company A's products. However, if a customer decides to drop one of the products they are no longer eligible to receive the 10 percent discount on the other products.

Now let's say you are a new venture that wants to break in to this market by selling a single competing product to a customer that buys four products from Company A. If the customer wants to try your new product, then there's a 10 percent increase in price on the other three products that the customer currently buys from Company A. Therefore to sell one product to the customer, you may have to price it at 40 percent below the market rate for that single product. Normally this is difficult for a new venture to do. Unless the venture can immediately supply all four products like the competition (Company A), breaking into the market will be very difficult. This is an exercise in incremental economics—and a very difficult competitive hurdle to overcome.

This plan is very close to the edge of legality in some states, depending on exact structure and language, and legal advice should be obtained before setting up such a marketing strategy. From the purchasing side, this practice is called "bundling" of supply contracts, and is a difficult thing for new ventures to deal with. For further reading see "Contract 'Bundling' Keeps Small Firms Away," by Jeff Bailey, page B4, *Wall Street Journal*, Tuesday, Oct 8, 2002.

PRICING AND SALES STRATEGIES

In many cases a new venture will need to expedite early sales to generate cash flow. Informed pricing and sales strategies can minimize the time required to enter a market or to reduce marketing costs.

Sales Strategies

Selling through a distributor

A primary advantage of selling through a distributor is that a retail network is already in place. This means lower marketing costs and immediate sales for the start-up. Also, the distributor can be an excellent source of market research, by way of volume and pricing information. The disadvantages are that your selling price is much lower, and you do not get direct customer feedback. Building a retail sales force and a network of retail customers may never be practical in some situations.

Selling through manufacturer's representatives or brokers

A manufacturer's representative is usually an independent contractor who makes a living by marketing equipment for many different companies. In many cases the "rep" is a former salesperson or purchasing agent in a specific field, who has many personal contacts and a "network" to exploit. They usually have the ability to see many purchasing agents and have instant credibility with these agents, and can speed market entry. They are usually a good source of market research, but sometimes feel that this is the source of their income and are reluctant to share much market feedback.

Licensing technology rather than manufacturing a product yourself

This is a good way for a small organization with few resources to get started. The venture is essentially a stand-alone R&D company that makes money from its technical developments, and leaves manufacturing and selling to others. Obviously the costs are low, but most of the profit may go to the company who takes the manufacturing and sales risks. It is difficult to get customer feedback here as well.

Forming a strategic partnership with a larger company

This is a variation or combination of the first three. Essentially you are using your venture for product development and a larger company for manufacturing and distribution, and then sharing the profits. This is particularly common for high development cost or high liability-profile products, such as pharmaceuticals or biotech products.

All of these techniques will allow quicker market entry and less-extensive marketing efforts, but all come with some sacrifice of market feedback and overall profit.

Note: Never use more than one of the above techniques at a time. You do not want to end up competing with yourself or confusing the market by having more than one person selling your product.

Pricing

Pricing is a matter of judgment, market research, and strategy. Pricing should be determined independent of cost of manufacture, and should be maximized based on what the market will bear.

Contract pricing is a complex subject and requires professional legal review. The primary problem with contract pricing is finding a mechanism to allow pricing to reflect market and economic changes over the contract period.

Setting contract prices with escalators from common indexes

Many annual supply contracts have pricing adjustments based on a factor of common indices, like the Consumer Price Index or published raw material costs, such as those published in the *Wall Street Journal* or *Platt's Oilgram News*. In some cases annual raw material purchasing and sales contracts are set on the same index, to provide some stable profitability.

Volume price discounts

In many cases costs of development and overhead are covered by the primary sales volumes, while incremental sales can be made that are still profitable at a lower pricing level. For example, the contract may state that the first 100,000 items are sold at $10 each and the next 100,000 purchased in the same year will be sold at $9 each. So, $1 of the sales price is used to cover fixed costs like salaries. Once these fixed costs are covered then additional sales can be sold at the $9 lower price while keeping the original profit margin. This is an attempt to gain market share while still selling at profitable levels. It is an excellent strategy for larger companies to use to make it hard for start-up ventures to enter a market. Note that you must have very good information on your variable operating costs to make a sophisticated judgment on volume price discounts.

Note: No contract can foresee all changes or contingencies to be covered. Be very careful in requiring your customer to fulfill contract provisions when you know it is a hardship (we call this "hammering" your customer or supplier). Remember, you will want another contract with this customer in the future and need his goodwill for long-term business.

OTHER MARKETING COMMENTS

Stay close to your customers. You are dependent upon your relationship with them to get market research data and to know when competition is trying to take your sales position. You cannot stay close to your customer by spending time in your office. Get out and see them in person. More information can be obtained in casual settings and by watching body language than in any amount of phone calls.

Know your competition. Go to all trade shows, and spend time researching your competition. You must know your competition to maximize your marketing effort and strategy. Know them better than they know you.

Negotiate any deals directly with a decision maker. We adopted a nickname for the person who has decision-making authority. We call this person "Oscar" for convenience. Many negotiations with customers where decision makers are not present end up being a waste of time. You are at a serious disadvantage negotiating with people of limited authority, because you can commit to concessions, but the customer's representative cannot. Negotiating with anyone other than Oscar leads to wasted time, agreements that are cancelled at higher levels, and one-sided arrangements. Try to find out who Oscar is for each customer, and make sure he is included in the final negotiations.

Note: I would strongly encourage you to attend a class on negotiations. This is a necessary survival skill that can be learned, and there are some good one- or two-day classes on this subject.

Final marketing/sales note: Advertising to increase sales is a very industry-specific subject and requires some help from professionals. I will not attempt to cover it in this book.

9

Characteristics of Successful Ventures

For the past twenty years I've been involved in dozens of ventures, either personally or as a consultant. In my judgment there are characteristics that are common to successful ventures. For your benefit, here are the ones I deem most important:

- **Top people who do not think they are above the petty details or who only want to study grand strategies.** Top people need to flip from the "forest" to the "trees" as necessary, because strategies evolve quickly in a new venture. A good grasp of operating details is necessary to quickly evolve strategies in crises.

- **Principals who have the ability to think and act "long term," even while "fighting fires."** It's critical to keep focused on the overall plan and goals, and to not lose direction with short-term "fixes." This problem often shows up as cash is running short.

- **A bias for action.** Speed of evolution is critical to success and preservation of cash. Inaction caused by too much studying, internal strife, or need to have perfect information can be fatal. Remember, if you are not a little nervous about taking an action, you probably waited too long to act. It is better to make ten decisions, some of which may have to be modified, rather than to spend the same time making one perfect decision.

- **Adequate cash and a passion to conserve cash at all times.** Lack of cash is the number one cause of venture failure. Have a culture of cash conservation and frugality, even when it does not seem critical for survival. Spend your cash on development or operations, not on non-operational items like fancy offices or other ego-satisfying possessions.

- **Speedy change and adaptation to development.** Rapid evolution through the development stage and into operations is critical to minimize cash usage and to stay in front of the competition.

- **Thorough knowledge of the competition.** A detailed knowledge of the competition is required for strategic planning and for marketing strategy. Do not expend resources competing where you do not have fundamental competitive advantages.

- **Knowledge of the technical and competitive advantages of the product.** Most sales and marketing today are technically based. Even commodities are differentiated on small technical or performance differences. It is beneficial if most of the management can articulate the technical advantages of products.

- **The intellectual honesty to admit (internally to the organization) weaknesses in products or the organization.** It's far better to address shortcomings within your organization than be surprised when the competition and customers point them out.

- **A culture of honesty.** Act honorably and honestly with customers, or they will go to your competitors. There's a huge pipeline of information that flows between customers and purchasing agents, particularly when there are product shortages. If your messages are inconsistent, then there's bound to be a loss of credibility and professional reputation. Always keep employees informed. They need to know how they are contributing to your success—that they are part of your team. Also, never lie to employees. It destroys morale and seems to make it OK for them to lie to you. Mark Twain once said, "Always do what's right; it will gratify some and astonish the rest." Employ visions and values and live by them. The public is cynical with good reason: corporate and government scandals hit the front page every day. Honesty is a strategic competitive advantage in this kind of climate. See comments for management concerning this subject in chapter ten.

- **Excellent accounting and management information systems.** These systems allow you to control all aspects of cash and production and they are critical to managing your business.

- **Reliance on budgets.** Creating a budget is an intellectual discipline that makes you plan for all aspects of the future. The discipline and process is as important as the final product.

- **Solid administrative controls.** Proper procedures must be in place for check signing, purchasing or expense commitment, and accounts payable approval. You must have these in place to have control of cash outlays.

- **Principals that are in charge.** Control of company direction, strategy, and products must be in the hands of the venture's principals. Loss of this control to outsiders, whether bankers or venture capitalists, will slow down decision making and the evolution of the company. This is another reason to be obsessed with cash conservation—to minimize possibility of loss of control and dilution of equity.

- **A willingness to share "the financial fun" very low in the organization.** Again, the best motivation is to keep employees fully informed so they are an integral part of achieving the venture's goals. Profit sharing programs, options, and other incentive pay tied to the profitability of the company are important for maintaining motivation, and are a characteristic of successful ventures.

- **Red tape cut to the bone.** Having short communication paths for decisions is critical to the speed of evolution. This includes decisions among principals and between principals and employees at all levels.

- **An excellent marketing strategy.** This plan is in continuous evolution, taking into account customer feedback and competitor strategies.

- **Application of the highest ethical standards.** Talking about ethics is useless unless your organization lives by what it says. There's no better example than Enron and WorldCom of how corporate malfeasance can lead to financial collapse affecting employees and shareholders. Honesty and integrity are the foundations of corporate success.

- **A reliance on operating excellence, rather than an overreliance on protection of intellectual property.** Intellectual property is critical to success, and should be protected diligently. However, intellectual property like patents, material sources, and manufacturing techniques will be seen or "rediscovered" by competitors sooner or later. The best insurance for venture success is operational excellence, or using operations as a strategic competitive advantage. If you are the most efficient or lowest-cost producer, then you can still compete and be successful, even if all your patents are circumvented or trade information is disclosed. You should strive for this position and continually evolve operational efficiency to stay in front of competitors.

- **Excellence in operations or execution as a strategic advantage.** Not enough is said about the need for excellence in operations or execution of daily business. This is the most important aspect of continuing success that I know. It is not the most glamorous, just the most important. Attention to detail is the key here, and the principal in charge of operations must have this critical ability. Allow me to reiterate: Entrepreneurship and successful ventures aren't about developing one "killer" application, product, or idea. They're about profitable daily operations that require making hundreds of small decisions, correctly, year in and year out.

- **Quality control is a high operational priority.** It is difficult to get that first sale to a new customer. The future of continued sales is often dependent upon the first shipment of product or service. The first shipment will receive much greater scrutiny than normal, and any defect may cause the entire marketing effort to fail. Once the initial product is rejected, it is difficult to get that image from the minds of purchasing agents or senior executives of the customer.

- **People who learn from (and admit) mistakes.** One of the best techniques for survival is to learn from your mistakes. This seems simple, but most people are reluctant to admit that a mistake was made, and as a consequence, they make it again and retard their evolution.

- **A venture is as strong as its weakest link.** Do not get caught thinking that strong technical expertise is the primary key to commercial success. Your ability to make a profit long term is the key to success and requires that all facets of the business operate well. Excellence across all operations is required.

- **Bonuses lead to focused incentives.** Bonus philosophy could take up a whole section of any management book. My philosophy covers these few simple areas. Successful companies usually have bonus plans that provide an incentive for the employee to increase the profitability of the venture. Basing part of an employee's bonus on profitability of the venture keeps everyone focused on the "bottom line" and does not give rise to false or "local" optimums. For instance I have seen bonuses for sales executives that were based on the increase in sales from one year to the next. This gives the employee incentives to raise sales without regard to profitability, or to cut prices to increase sales volumes even though the incremental sales may lose money. Never set up a system where the employee does well when the venture does not.

In larger organizations, with different divisions or profit centers, I have usually seen bonuses based only on the performance of the division. The philosophy here is to exactly align the bonus basis with the employee's area of responsibility. This also leads to "local" optimums, where the division is optimized rather than the entire company. I have seen cases where it costs the parent company $2 in lost profits for every $1 in increased profits at the division, leading to a net loss for the company, but a bigger bonus for the division employee. The practice of giving bonuses based on divisional performance is widespread, especially in organizations like integrated oil companies, and usually leads to poor relations between divisions as executives selfishly optimize their divisions and compete internally for profit splits and capital dollars.

The solution is to always be sure that some part of the bonus is based on the overall company profitability, which encourages interdivisional cooperation. I also recommend that part of the bonus basis be based on discretionary items, like how well the employee trained new hires, or how well the employee shared information. Many employees tend to hoard information, thinking that it makes them invaluable or gives them power.

The ultimate bonus that emphasizes overall company profitability is stock options, or in some cases, awards of stock. However, I recommend that all (or a large part of) options or stock awards be restricted either in vesting or in ability to sell. The purchase and sale of options should never be allowed in the same year. To do otherwise gives rise to the "Enron syndrome," where senior executives have an incentive to "pump" or falsify quarterly earnings to get the stock price up, so they can exercise and sell options before resigning. Some or all of the options or stock should not be salable for years to encourage long-term thinking in people. This one change would have vastly reduced the incentives for the WorldCom and Enron cheating. If options or stock awards are unavailable due to the size of the company, then I recommend a profit sharing plan that makes all employees feel that they share in the good and bad times of the company.

10

Management Tenets of Successful Ventures

A new venture will be built on thousands of important decisions in the first years of operation. The successful venture will need innovative technology and superior operations management to sell a product and make a profit. The management team that makes these decisions will make or break the company. As we've discussed in previous chapters, the best managers are those who learn from experience, both positive and negative. There are, however, tenets of successful ventures that appear time and again, which this chapter covers along with my own preferences of style and procedure.

- **Establish a corporate culture of honesty and integrity.** Management should take the lead in establishing a culture of honesty, integrity, and justice. Employees watch management for clues as to how to behave and treat customers. A culture of cheating or injustice will send a message that it is OK to cheat or steal from the company or customers. Employees are much more likely to treat management and customers with honesty and integrity if they are treated with respect, honesty, and justice. You cannot manage your business if employees rationalize that it is OK to steal or lie because they have seen someone in management do it.

- **Use management authority wisely.** The top leadership of the company, particularly the president or CEO, is in a position of power. The office has the authority to make decisions that profoundly affect a venture. The corollary to power is a responsibility to use authority with discretion. The country's most celebrated management teacher, Peter Drucker, once wrote that good management isn't about "doing things right," but about "doing the right things." Efficiency is not the same as effectiveness. Top management's primary role is to set the direction of the company, both today and tomorrow. Leadership however is compromised when there's an adversarial relationship between top managers and subordinates. If a

CEO has to say "do it my way because I said so, and I'm the boss," then the CEO and the venture are in trouble.

Spend as much time as possible to persuade your people to be committed to an agreed-upon course of action, so that the momentum is in one direction. My philosophy is that managers are enablers. Their main job is to provide resources and remove obstacles for the men and women working for them. At other times this also means rolling up sleeves and working side by side with subordinates, or filling in when extra "horsepower" is suddenly required in an area.

- **Put the interests of the organization first.** Lead by example by putting the organization first. Personal acclaim and financial reward will follow from the venture's success. This is the central theme of an excellent book, *Good to Great,* by Jim Collins. It's a must-read for anyone running any company of any size. Personally, I hope that every CEO will read this book and bring the era of the overpaid "rock star" CEO to an end.

- **Let your people share in the success.** To ensure that people feel like they are part of the team, and to provide motivation, share the credit for successes freely. Compliment people for their accomplishments often, and do it in front of others. You can provide necessary fulfillment to an employee, and it is a lot cheaper than a pay increase. You should also allow employees to share in the financial success of the company, so that everyone "wins" when the company "wins." See the section on bonus structures in chapter nine.

- **Don't try to do everything yourself.** The job of upper management is to set direction and to provide the resources so that employees can do their job quickly and efficiently. Never be the reason that employees have to wait to do their work or are unable to perform their job duties. Do not get bogged down by trying to micromanage every crisis. The last thing you want to do is to jump in and do someone's job, while everyone else is standing around without resources or direction. As you get larger, you will do more managing and less "doing." If you cannot evolve with this, find professional managers to do the managing.

- **Human engineer the jobs.** This is not an exhortation to cloning. It means that the jobs should be designed with incentives that align the best interests of the employee and the venture. Never build a job or incentives such that the success of the employee depends on the failure of the organization or vice versa.

- **Regularly assess fundamental competitive weaknesses (and strengths).** Informal strategy sessions should routinely assess fundamental competitive strengths and weaknesses. Both of these should be used in evolving marketing and product development strategy and direction. For example, having only two products may put you at a disadvantage compared to a competitor who has five, but funding multiple development schemes may bankrupt the company. Perhaps the marketing list should then be reduced to only those companies who don't need all five product lines. In other words don't try to compete where you are at a fundamental disadvantage and probability of failure is high. To do so is a waste of resources, and will slow your evolution in a successful direction. There is a reason why you do not see antelopes challenging lions for territory: they are almost always killed and eaten. Remember your successful evolution strategies.

  My business partner and I set a goal to have lunch at least three days a week, just to address strategy and competition, and update our "rolling" strategic plan. A weekly or monthly informal review is probably the very minimum required.

- **Plan Diligently and Execute Violently.** This is an excellent mental image of how to operate. Basically this means that you should plan very carefully, and look at possible problems and downsides. However, once you decide on a plan, you should execute the plan with as much energy and speed as possible. The planning phase does not consume cash as rapidly as the execution phase. Once you get to the execution phase, you must run as fast as you can until successful.

  Note: During start-up you will run out of cash quickly unless managers lead you to profitable operations, so get operations and accounting/financial managers on your team early. Also, remember that it's difficult to teach creativity and good judgment, so hang on to good people with these skills when you find them.

- **Have a bias for action.** Speed of evolution to profitable operations is critical. Have a bias for action and making decisions as quickly as possible. In most cases, if you are very comfortable taking an action, then you have probably waited too long. There is a fine line between making a rash judgment and taking bold action that will put you in front of competition. If you are a procrastinator by nature, entrepreneurship is probably not for you. This is repeated from the previous chapter for emphasis.

- **Live by the numbers.** Pay attention to the numbers in your budgets and monthly financials. This is the only objective way to judge the progress of the venture. In the early days, pay very close attention to cash forecasts and rate of cash consumption (burn rate). Many ventures can show profitability while having negative cash flow. Many can also show positive cash flow with negative profitability. You can run indefinitely with the second condition (positive cash flow), but not with the first. You must be able to discern which condition you have. Inability to project cash requirements will probably lead to cash and venture failures. A good budget and accounting system should allow you to judge your success on a weekly, if not daily, basis. You will live or die by these numbers, so keep them accurate and close.

- **Do it within the organization.** Whenever possible, try to perform necessary action items with internal resources (do it internally and save money). Not only will this cut down on expensive outside professional fees (and save cash!), but also it will build internal expertise that can be used again. For example, you can pay an attorney to keep your corporate record book and issue stock certificates, or you can do it yourself and let an attorney review your work, at much less cost. This requires some judgment and experience to know what you should attempt (and what you should not). Try to get some help from experienced directors or other sources.

- **Find sources of free expertise.** Gather all the free expertise you can from experienced sources or mentors. This is one reason I have a bias for using angel investors, rather than large VC companies, for funding. Usually you can get similar terms on funding, but you can usually get the angel investor very involved in decision making at no extra cost. Most angel investors have "been there and done that" many times. Another source of expertise is retired executives from the same industry. Many of them will consult as a way to keep their juices flowing, and may not charge much or need the money.

- **Be Adaptable.** You must constantly adapt to a changing environment. Pay attention to the signals the market is sending. Like any species, if you do not adapt quickly, you will become extinct. Adaptation in a corporate sense means constantly reassessing your strategic plan and reacting to changes in your marketplace and competition.

- **Act with honesty and integrity.** Ethical conduct is critically important to good relationships with employees and customers, and is the foundation of a successful venture. A culture of justice and fairness for employees and customers are keys to retaining both. Act well, and you'll sleep better. You will have plenty of other things to lose sleep over.

- **Encourage two-way communications.** Ross Perot has a saying: "Listen, listen, listen to the people doing the work." Listen to your employees. You may be amazed at what you learn about your company or yourself. Communicate downward, especially about how the company is doing financially. Such communications should not include confidential information that competitors could use, but should serve as indicators of your respect and trust in your employees.

  If you treat employees with courtesy and respect, communications will flow much more easily. Nothing is more threatening to long-term survival than unmotivated or adversarial employees. You will find that adversarial employees will actually say negative things about the company to clients to "get even." This is a path to venture failure. Be sure they tell you the negative things before they tell the clients and customers.

- **Practice what you preach.** This may sound overly simplistic, but it has broad implications. Doing what you say you will is necessary to build credibility with, and loyalty from, customers. It also provides a secure platform for your employees to comfortably do their jobs without hesitating from insecurity. Remember, hesitation leads to slow evolution, which is a prescription for failure.

11

Common Reasons for Venture Failures

I hate to end this book with a discussion on failures. Think of this chapter not just as a way to avoid failure, but also as a way to ensure success. We have seen the "good" and read about the "ugly"; now comes the "bad." Venture failure is very bad for everybody.

Venture failures are ultimately caused by running out of cash ("cash failure"). There are many causes for running out of cash, but cash failure is the end of your venture. Period. Be watchful for the following, as they are some of the main causes of failure.

CONTRIBUTORS TO CASH FLOW PROBLEMS

Profitable, but negative cash flow

Earlier we discussed the difference between profitability and cash flow. One of the common causes for cash failure is being lulled into a false sense of financial upswing by an income statement that shows the venture is profitable, when in actuality it has had unnoticed negative cash flow for an extended period. The negative cash flow could be caused by inventory or accounts receivable buildup or other non-income items.

Failure to control accounts receivable

This amounts to giving customers an interest-free loan. The longer a venture allows the A/R aging to increase, the greater the odds that the A/R will not be collectable and will have to be written off. Pressuring overdue customers is an unpleasant job and human nature is to procrastinate. Procrastination can lead to cash failure.

Failure to control inventory levels

Paying for inventory buildup will not show up on the income statement, but will use cash. It's part of what is referred to as "working funds." When cash is "tight," increasing inventory can use cash necessary for payroll or other operations.

Failure to meet loan covenants

Almost all banks have loan covenants, or clauses specifying conditions under which they can cancel or "call" the loan. Usually these clauses are based on ratios, such as total debt to book value or ratios of certain assets to liabilities. Typically banks give warnings of covenant violations, but repeated or egregious violations can cause the banks to make a preemptive strike to get as much assets as possible to minimize losses. If a bank feels it has to call the loans, it is usually fatal to the venture.

LAWSUITS

Lawsuits come in many shapes and sizes, but all can lead to cash and venture failure. The following sources of lawsuits are just a sample:

- Massive product or quality control (QC) failure, leading to extensive recall or product replacement
- Environmental problems
- Workplace injury/personal injury
- Intellectual property disputes
- Employee lying or other malfeasance

Lawsuits are unpredictable. Even a successful defense can cause so much management distraction and expense that a venture is forced into bankruptcy protection. Part of the problem is sheer volume and complexity of regulations. It's hard to imagine any of the Fortune 500 companies that are in full compliance with all state and federal OSHA regulations, even though they apply huge amounts of personnel to these issues. Small ventures simply do not have the resources to know the standards, much less meet them, no matter how well intentioned. I therefore strongly recommend that your venture do everything it can to stay out of the courthouse.

CASE STUDY: DIRT TECHNOLOGY, LLC

One additional experience from Dirt Technology might be instructive here.

We had a terrible tragedy befall us when a motorcyclist ran into the back of one of our delivery trucks. The motorcycle driver was killed. The family of the motorcycle driver hired attorneys and sued our company for $2 million.

Fortunately, if I can actually use that term here, we sent investigators out to take pictures and interview people while the police were there. The investigation showed that the motorcycle was traveling between 80 and 100 miles per hour in a 35-mile-per-hour zone and was attempting to pass our truck that was turning left. This did not deter the lawsuit or the plaintiff's attorney, who told us that he would put the motorcycle driver's mother and sister on the stand, and they would cry, and the jury would want to help them. He also informed us that people did not like trucks, the companies that owned them, or insurance companies, and that the family would win in spite of who was "wrong."

Well, we went to court and won, but it still cost our insurance company over $100,000, an expense which was passed on to us over the next three years.

There is a bias against companies and trucks in our society, so be very careful about going to court. Even "winning" could put you out of business.

OPERATING MISTAKES OR HIGH-RISK ACTIONS CAN LEAD TO SUDDEN OPERATIONAL FAILURE

There are some activities or operational decisions that are highly risky and should be avoided. I particularly recommend avoiding the following:

- **Outsourcing critical operations, such as QC, final production, or sales.** Although other operations can be successfully outsourced, failure of these operations will put you out of business. You cannot trust outsiders to spend the time or to have the knowledge of priorities to carry out these operations. You need to develop this experience internally to be viable.

- **Single sourcing of a critical resource.** Single sourcing of a necessary raw material is dangerous, and is a prescription for insomnia until the situation is remedied. Even an "ironclad" supply contract is subject to disasters and "acts of God" that can wipe a supplier's production facility out for years. Find a backup supplier, even if you have to pay more or have to guarantee a secondary supplier a portion of your business to induce them to produce the resource.

- **High concentration of sales to a single customer.** High dependence on one or two large customers is ill advised, as it will lead to a sudden reduction in sales and cash in the event that the customer is lost. If your venture cannot avoid this situation, try diligently to get annual supply contracts with six-month notice provisions. At least this will give the venture time to react or downsize accordingly. Note that high dependence on one customer makes your venture particularly vulnerable to a competitor using a stealth market entry marketing strategy. Stay very close to these large customers to avoid being surprised.

- **Failure to pay required federal or state taxes.** Failure to deposit federal taxes (941 payments) or state sales taxes on time may be fatal. The penalties on late payments are onerous (up to an immediate 10 percent; see IRS Web site for details). You will eventually have to pay these penalties, plus interest, to stay in business. The IRS has the power to seize bank accounts and other assets, whereas other vendors and creditors do not. Pay the IRS and state sales taxes first, no matter what else has to be postponed.

- **Failure to keep corporate structure intact.** Loss of your corporate structure, or failure to keep your corporate veil intact, can lead to loss of corporate charter. This can lead to owners being personally responsible for corporate liabilities. This means that the owners could be wiped out personally in the event of a corporate lawsuit that occurs when the company is out of compliance with the state. Be sure to keep your registered agent address current so that any notices of loss of compliance are received and acted upon. Failure to pay state income, franchise, or sales taxes is often a fatal error, and can lead to massive personal exposure. Also, mingling corporate and personal funds or checking accounts can allow lawyers to take personal assets to pay for corporate debts.

- **Failure to do due diligence on acquisitions or strategic partners.** Due diligence* is a term used to cover inquiries into another company's business health and practices. Failure to audit the accounting or legal liabilities of a potential acquisition or possible strategic partner can be fatal or lead to lawsuits from minority stockholders claiming breach of fiduciary responsibilities or negligence—just as bad is partnering with someone of questionable ethics or reputation. Loss of your reputation by association can be just as fatal as if you caused the loss of reputation yourself.

* *"Due diligence" is a technical and legal/accounting exercise, and you should get professional help to understand the term and responsibilities involved.*

Cash failure is the usual result of many of the items I have described. Once again, use your accounting software and budgets to give you early warnings of a cash crisis. And remember the first rule of project and venture development work: everything is likely to take twice as long and cost twice as much as you think it should.

Lesson: Keep some cash sources available for the unexpected! You should now be obsessive about cash retention!

We have come to the end of the lessons, evolutionary moments, and advice. You should be saturated with entrepreneurial knowledge at this point. It is time to go out and be successful! I do, however, have some final thoughts for you in the epilogue.

Epilogue

The original purpose for writing this book was defensive in nature. As an entrepreneur-in-residence at the University of Texas, I volunteer my time (up to a point) for engineers, scientists, and MBAs that want to start a new venture. I started writing these ideas down so I would not have to repeat them each time. The idea was to give each of them a copy, and tell them to take an aspirin, read the notes, and call me in the morning, to save me time.

A broader vision emerged as I wrote, that of being a service to society by helping more ventures survive the start-up years. The U.S. economy is changing and reacting to globalization forces. We must find a way to compete with low-cost foreign workers to keep our standard of living. The United States is highly competitive when we combine our business and technical skills with our ability to be creative and take risks. The world cannot compete (yet) with our unique ability to commercialize innovative technologies and consumer ideas. As a country we cannot afford to be wasting money on failed start-ups. Failed start-ups are a drag, whereas successful start-ups provide new jobs and material benefits to society. I hope the information in this book leads to increased numbers of successful start-ups, along with the resulting benefits to society.

Also, the venture capital world is changing, with VCs being more demanding on the deals they will finance. They also are more reluctant to finance companies before they have management and operations in place. Many of them would like to become more like private equity companies, where there is less risk. This is another reason to try low cash start-ups. The farther you can evolve toward operations, the more equity you can retain. The *Wall Street Journal* has even written stories on companies trying to skip the VC-funding stage and go directly from low cash start-up and operation to sale to a public company. Go as far as you can with your own money to retain more equity in the final entity.

I hope I have not overly frightened any of you with all the forms, "tall tales," and details of a start-up. Sometimes you wonder how anybody can actually survive all the trials of setting up a new company. All of you will probably come out with a new appreciation for the need for justice system (tort) reform and for the need to remove state and federal impediments to business development. Our legislators are predominantly lawyers with little background in business or economics. They often have good intentions, but frequently pass regulations that have terrible consequences. They need our input, but it is difficult to find time for this when you are surviving a start-up. We must have their help to remain competitive in a globalized economy.

Finally, if you are successful in your endeavors, take time afterward to help another person start a new venture. The world will be a better place for your effort.

My last advice is to save your cash where you can, keep your trucks out of septic tanks, and remember: in your life and in your venture, it is the journey that is important. Have some fun along the way!

Bruce Thornton

Glossary

Accounts payable	A list of amounts of money owed to suppliers and vendors for goods or services purchased
Accounts receivable	A list of amounts of money owed by each customer, and how many days it has been owed (for credit sales)
Angel investor	An individual investor, usually experienced in the business area in question; a source of funding and management help
Articles of incorporation	A legal document stating the purpose and business area of a corporation
Capital budget	An estimate of capital (equipment) purchases, usually for an annual period
C-corporation	A legal organization for larger companies—dividends and profits are both taxed
Confidentiality agreement	See NDA
Corporate document book	A collection of corporate forms, meeting minutes, and legal documents needed to be in compliance with state government regulations
Credit application	A form to be sent to customers stating terms of credit sales and requesting references to check creditworthiness
Depreciation	A type of expense against earnings to reflect the declining value of equipment as it wears out

EIN	Employer's Identification Number, used by a company to report wages and withholding taxes to the federal government
Equity (or cash) calls	The activity of calling for more money from existing equity (stock) holders
Equity financing	The activity of obtaining money for a business by selling stock
Evolutionary moment	A critical decision point where it is necessary to evaluate whether to proceed with the venture or whether to revise growth direction
Gross profit	Total sales revenue minus the cost of goods sold
Hammering	An attempt to enforce specific contract performance, possibly even when fairness is in question
HOGs	Acronym for Helpful Old Guys or an experienced businessperson
Limited Liability Company (LLC)	A legal organization that provides liability protection for owners like a corporation but which is taxed like a partnership (similar to S-corporation)
Limited Liability Partnership (LLP)	A legal organization like an LLC but usually for professionals like doctors or lawyers
Management	The activity of coordinating all employees and work in a company
Marketing	The activity of planning the strategy of sales, pricing, and product lines
NDA	Nondisclosure Agreement or agreement to keep information confidential
Net profit	Total sales revenue minus cost of goods sold, minus operating expenses, usually before income taxes are assessed

Operating budget	An estimate of future sales and expenses resulting in a net profit estimate, usually for twelve monthly periods
Oscar	A nickname for a person who has final authority in a negotiation
Personal guarantee	A pledge to a lender that an individual owner will personally repay the loan if the business or corporation defaults on the loan
Price vs. volume elasticity	The relationship between demand for goods and the change in sales that occurs as the price is changed: usually lower price means more sales
Product development	The evolutionary activity of turning an idea into a product for sale to the marketplace
Sales	The activity of executing the marketing strategy and maintenance of customers
Sales tax exemption	A form issued by the state that allows materials to be legally purchased or sold without paying state sales or use tax
S-corporation	A legal organization for smaller companies: profit is taxed one time, directly to the stockholders
Secretary of state	A state organization that regulates commercial activities including corporations and corporate registrations
Signature loans	Loans not collateralized by equipment or goods, but based solely on a promise to pay
State comptroller	The state office responsible for state taxation and collection
State charter	The document issued by the state making a corporation legal
Toll processing	The activity of paying a custom manufacturer to make your product
TWC	Texas Workforce Commission: handles state employment and unemployment taxes

Venture capitalist
(VC)   Investment company that specializes in funding new ventures; source of funding at stages of venture development

Workers'
compensation   A state regulated insurance program for worker death and injury payments; this insurance has statutory limits on employer liability

Working funds   Money needed to buy inventory and to finance accounts receivable (credit sales)

Working line of credit A loan secured by inventory and customer accounts receivable; usually fluctuates monthly depending on inventory and sales levels

Appendix

Disclaimer: The forms and examples in the appendix are included as examples only. They should not be used without consulting the proper legal or accounting professionals. Most of the forms are available online at the Web sites listed.

PART 1
FORMS FOR INITIAL ORGANIZATION

1. **Confidentiality agreement**

2. **Employee nondisclosure agreement (NDA)**

3. **Articles of organization for an LLC**

4. **Articles of incorporation for a corporation**

5. **IRS form SS-4: Application for Employer Identification Number (EIN)**

6. **List of Useful Web Sites**

Example

Confidentiality Agreement

This confidentiality agreement is made and entered into on October 16, 2006, by, and between Dirt Technology, LLC, hereinafter known as "DIRT") and the XXXXXX Company (hereinafter known as "XXXXXX").

BACKGROUND

DIRT and XXXXXX have expressed a desire to exchange information relative to their various business activities, and specifically information concerning material sources, manufacture, and sales of horticultural materials.

The parties believe that it is essential that certain information be exchanged in order for them to continue their discussions regarding the foregoing matters. For purposes of this agreement, the information provided by DIRT shall hereinafter be referred to as the "DIRT Information" and the information by XXXXXX shall hereinafter be referred to as the "XXXXXX Information."

In consideration of the mutual desire to exchange information and to proceed with discussions as described above, the parties hereto agree as follows:

1. Confidentiality of Information

a.) The DIRT Information and the XXXXXX Information shall be kept confidential by the other party and shall not, without prior written consent, be disclosed in any manner whatsoever, in whole or in part, and shall not be used for any purpose other than the subject purpose.

b.) The DIRT Information and the XXXXXX Information shall only be revealed to those agents or employees of the other party which need to know the Information for purposes of the subject purpose and shall inform each person to whom the Information is disclosed of its confidential nature.

c.) Both parties shall be responsible for any breach of this agreement by its agents, employees, or contractors.

d.) Neither party shall disclose, without the written consent of the other, the fact that Information has been made available to them, the existence of any negotiations between the parties with regard to the subject purpose, or any of the terms, conditions or other facts with respect to the subject purpose, including the status thereof. Such negotiations shall remain strictly private and confidential as between the parties, except to the extent required by applicable law and except as reasonably necessary to accomplish the objective contemplated hereunder.

2. Term of the Agreement

This agreement shall remain in full force and effect until the expiration of a period of five years from and after the date of execution hereof, unless earlier terminated by the mutual agreement of the parties in writing.

3. Miscellaneous

a.) This agreement shall be governed by and construed in accordance with the laws of the state of Texas.

b.) The term "Information" does not include information that (i) becomes generally available to the public; (ii) was available on a non-confidential basis prior to its disclosure; or (iii) corresponds in substance to information independently developed by employees of the other party, who have not had access to the information.

c.) This agreement is intended as the final expression of both parties and is the complete and exclusive statement thereof. No statements or agreements, oral or written, made prior to or at the time of signing hereof, shall vary or modify the written terms hereof; and neither party shall claim any amendment or release from any provision hereof by reason of a course of action or mutual agreement unless such agreement is in writing, signed by the other party and specifically stating it as an amendment to the agreement.

d.) If any provision herein is or becomes invalid or illegal, in whole or in part, such provision shall be deemed amended, as nearly as possible, to be consistent with the intent expressed in this agreement, and if such is impossible, that provision shall fall by itself without invalidating any of the remaining provisions not otherwise invalid or illegal.

In witness whereof, this agreement is executed in duplicate originals as of the date above.

Dirt Technology, LLC   XXXXXX

By: _____   By: _____

Employee Nondisclosure Agreement

Dirt Technology, LLC (DIRT) has confidential trade information, including, but not limited to:

- Prices for goods sold and for raw materials
- Customer lists
- Product formulas
- Business strategy
- Freight arrangements
- Strategic alliances with other businesses

It would be harmful to DIRT for anyone to divulge this information to competitors, customers, or anyone outside the company.

As a condition of my employment, I hereby agree not to directly or indirectly disclose to any other person or to use any of DIRT's confidential information or trade secrets except with DIRT's written permission. I additionally agree that DIRT's confidential information and trade secrets are DIRT's exclusive property and are not to be removed from DIRT's premises without DIRT's prior written approval. I further agree to return to DIRT any and all such confidential information and trade secrets to DIRT immediately upon demand.

Signed: _____

Date: _____

Articles of Organization for Limited Liability Company Formation (LLC)

Form 205 **(Revised 01/06)** Return in duplicate to: Secretary of State P.O. Box 13697 Austin, TX 78711-3697 512 463-5555 FAX: 512 463-5709 **Filing Fee: $300**	 **Certificate of Formation** **Limited Liability Company**	This space reserved for office use.

Article 1 – Entity Name and Type

The filing entity being formed is a limited liability company. The name of the entity is:

_____

The name must contain the words "limited liability company," "limited company," or an abbreviation of one of these phrases.

Article 2 – Registered Agent and Registered Office
(Select and complete either A or B and complete C)

☐ A. The initial registered agent is an organization (cannot be entity named above) by the name of:

_____

OR

☐ B. The initial registered agent is an individual resident of the state whose name is set forth below:

_____
First Name   *M.I.*   *Last Name*   *Suffix*

C. The business address of the registered agent and the registered office address is:

                                                                     TX

Street Address   *City*   *State*   *Zip Code*

Article 3 – Governing Authority
(Select and complete either A or B and provide the name and address of each governing person.)

☐ A. The limited liability company will have managers. The name and address of each initial manager are set forth below.

☐ B. The limited liability company will not have managers. The company will be governed by its members, and the name and address of each initial member are set forth below.

NAME OF GOVERNING PERSON (Enter the name of either an individual or an organization, but not both.)

IF INDIVIDUAL

First Name	*M.I.*	*Last Name*	*Suffix*

OR

IF ORGANIZATION

Organization Name

ADDRESS OF GOVERNING PERSON

Street or Mailing Address	*City*	*State*	*Country*	*Zip Code*

NAME OF GOVERNING PERSON (Enter the name of either an individual or an organization, but not both.)						
IF INDIVIDUAL						
First Name	M.I.	Last Name				Suffix
IF ORGANIZATION						
Organization Name						

OR

ADDRESS OF GOVERNING PERSON					
Street or Mailing Address		City	State	Country	Zip Code

NAME OF GOVERNING PERSON (Enter the name of either an individual or an organization, but not both.)						
IF INDIVIDUAL						
First Name	M.I.	Last Name				Suffix
IF ORGANIZATION						
Organization Name						

OR

ADDRESS OF GOVERNING PERSON					
Street or Mailing Address		City	State	Country	Zip Code

Article 4 – Purpose

The purpose for which the company is formed is for the transaction of any and all lawful purposes for which a limited liability company may be organized under the Texas Business Organizations Code.

Supplemental Provisions/Information

Text Area: [The attached addendum, if any, is incorporated herein by reference.]

Organizer

The name and address of the organizer:

_____
Name

_____
Street or Mailing Address   _City_   _State   Zip Code_

Effectiveness of Filing (Select either A, B, or C.)

A. ☐ This document becomes effective when the document is filed by the secretary of state.

B. ☐ This document becomes effective at a later date, which is not more than ninety (90) days from the date of signing. The delayed effective date is: _____

C. ☐ This document takes effect upon the occurrence of the future event or fact, other than the passage of time. The 90th day after the date of signing is: _____

The following event or fact will cause the document to take effect in the manner described below:

_____

_____

Execution

The undersigned signs this document subject to the penalties imposed by law for the submission of a materially false or fraudulent instrument.

Date: _____

_____
Signature of organizer

Form 205

Articles of Incorporation for a Corporation

Form 201 **(Revised 1/06)** Return in duplicate to: Secretary of State P.O. Box 13697 Austin, TX 78711-3697 512 463-5555 FAX: 512/463-5709 **Filing Fee: $300**	 **Certificate of Formation For-profit Corporation**	This space reserved for office use.

Article 1 – Entity Name and Type

The filing entity being formed is a for-profit corporation. The name of the entity is:

The name must contain the word "corporation," "company," "incorporated," "limited" or an abbreviation of one of these terms.

Article 2 – Registered Agent and Registered Office
(Select and complete either A or B and complete C)

☐ A. The initial registered agent is an organization (cannot be entity named above) by the name of:

OR

☐ B. The initial registered agent is an individual resident of the state whose name is set forth below:

First Name	*M.I.*	*Last Name*	*Suffix*

C. The business address of the registered agent and the registered office address is:

		TX	
Street Address	*City*	*State*	*Zip Code*

Article 3 – Directors
(A minimum of 1 director is required.)

The number of directors constituting the initial board of directors and the names and addresses of the person or persons who are to serve as directors until the first annual meeting of shareholders or until their successors are elected and qualified are as follows:

Director 1				
First Name	*M.I.*	*Last Name*		*Suffix*
Street or Mailing Address	*City*	*State*	*Zip Code*	*Country*

Director 2				
First Name	*M.I.*	*Last Name*		*Suffix*
Street or Mailing Address	*City*		*State*	*Zip Code*	*Country*

Director 3				
First Name	*M.I.*	*Last Name*		*Suffix*
Street or Mailing Address	*City*		*State*	*Zip Code*	*Country*

Article 4 – Authorized Shares
(Provide the number of shares in the space below, then select option A or option B, do not select both.)

The total number of shares the corporation is authorized to issue is: _____

☐ A. The par value of each of the authorized shares is: _____
OR

☐ B. The shares shall have no par value.

If the shares are to be divided into classes, you must set forth the designation of each class, the number of shares of each class, the par value (or statement of no par value), and the preferences, limitations, and relative rights of each class in the space provided for supplemental information on this form.

Article 5 – Purpose

The purpose for which the corporation is formed is for the transaction of any and all lawful business for which a for-profit corporation may be organized under the Texas Business Organizations Code.

Supplemental Provisions/Information

Text Area: [The attached addendum, if any, is incorporated herein by reference.]

Organizer

The name and address of the organizer:

_____
Name

_____
Street or Mailing Address   *City*   *State*   *Zip Code*

Effectiveness of Filing (Select either A, B, or C.)

A. ☐ This document becomes effective when the document is filed by the secretary of state.

B. ☐ This document becomes effective at a later date, which is not more than ninety (90) days from the date of signing. The delayed effective date is: _____

C. ☐ This document takes effect upon the occurrence of a future event or fact, other than the passage of time. The 90th day after the date of signing is: _____

The following event or fact will cause the document to take effect in the manner described below:

_____

_____

Execution

The undersigned signs this document subject to the penalties imposed by law for the submission of a materially false or fraudulent instrument.

Date: _____

_____
Signature of organizer

IRS form SS4 Application for EIN

Form **SS-4** (Rev. December 2001) Department of the Treasury Internal Revenue Service	**Application for Employer Identification Number** (For use by employers, corporations, partnerships, trusts, estates, churches, government agencies, Indian tribal entities, certain individuals, and others.) ▶ See separate Instructions for each line. ▶ Keep a copy for your records.	EIN OMB No. 1545-0003

	1 Legal name of entity (or individual) for whom the EIN is being requested

Type or print clearly.

2 Trade name of business (if different from name on line 1)	**3** Executor, trustee, "care of" name

4a Mailing address (room, apt., suite no. and street, or P.O. box)	**5a** Street address (if different) (Do not enter a P.O. box.)
4b City, state, and ZIP code	**5b** City, state, and ZIP code

6 County and state where principal business is located

7a Name of principal officer, general partner, grantor, owner, or trustor	**7b** SSN, ITIN, or EIN

8a Type of entity (check only one box)

☐ Sole proprietor (SSN) _____
☐ Partnership
☐ Corporation (enter form number to be filed) ▶ _____
☐ Personal service corp.
☐ Church or church-controlled organization
☐ Other nonprofit organization (specify) ▶ _____
☐ Other (specify) ▶

☐ Estate (SSN of decedent) _____
☐ Plan administrator (SSN) _____
☐ Trust (SSN of grantor) _____
☐ National Guard   ☐ State/local government
☐ Farmers' cooperative ☐ Federal government/military
☐ REMIC   ☐ Indian tribal governments/enterprises
Group Exemption Number (GEN) ▶

8b If a corporation, name the state or foreign country (if applicable) where incorporated — State _____ Foreign country _____

9 Reason for applying (check only one box)
☐ Started new business (specify type) ▶ _____
☐ Hired employees (Check the box and see line 12.)
☐ Compliance with IRS withholding regulations
☐ Other (specify) ▶

☐ Banking purpose (specify purpose) ▶ _____
☐ Changed type of organization (specify new type) ▶ _____
☐ Purchased going business
☐ Created a trust (specify type) ▶ _____
☐ Created a pension plan (specify type) ▶ _____

10 Date business started or acquired (month, day, year)   **11** Closing month of accounting year

12 First date wages or annuities were paid or will be paid (month, day, year). **Note:** *If applicant is a withholding agent, enter date income will first be paid to nonresident alien. (month, day, year)* . . . . ▶

13 Highest number of employees expected in the next 12 months. **Note:** *If the applicant does not expect to have any employees during the period, enter "-0-."* . . . . ▶	Agricultural	Household	Other

14 Check **one** box that best describes the principal activity of your business.
☐ Construction ☐ Rental & leasing ☐ Transportation & warehousing ☐ Accommodation & food service ☐ Wholesale-agent/broker
☐ Real estate ☐ Manufacturing ☐ Finance & insurance ☐ Other (specify) ☐ Health care & social assistance ☐ Wholesale-other ☐ Retail

15 Indicate principal line of merchandise sold; specific construction work done; products produced; or services provided.

16a Has the applicant ever applied for an employer identification number for this or any other business? . . . . ☐ Yes ☐ No
Note: *If "Yes," please complete lines 16b and 16c.*

16b If you checked "Yes" on line 16a, give applicant's legal name and trade name shown on prior application if different from line 1 or 2 above.
Legal name ▶ _____ Trade name ▶ _____

16c Approximate date when, and city and state where, the application was filed. Enter previous employer identification number if known.
Approximate date when filed (mo., day, year) _____ City and state where filed _____ Previous EIN _____

Third Party Designee	Complete this section **only** if you want to authorize the named individual to receive the entity's EIN and answer questions about the completion of this form.	
	Designee's name	Designee's telephone number (include area code) ( )
	Address and ZIP code	Designee's fax number (include area code) ( )

Under penalties of perjury, I declare that I have examined this application, and to the best of my knowledge and belief, it is true, correct, and complete.

Applicant's telephone number (include area code) ( )

Name and title (type or print clearly) ▶

Applicant's fax number (include area code) ( )

Signature ▶ _____ Date ▶ _____

For Privacy Act and Paperwork Reduction Act Notice, see separate instructions.   Cat. No. 16055N   Form **SS-4** (Rev. 12-2001)

List of Useful Web Sites

www.otc.utexas.edu Office of Technology Commercialization, University of Texas at Austin.

www.sos.state.tx.us Office of the Secretary of State, Texas. Keeps corporate records.

www.cpa.state.tx.us Office of the State Comptroller. Information on franchise and sales taxes.

www.twc.state.tx.us Texas Workforce Commission; for state ID number and SUTA deposits.

www.taxes.ca.gov/forms1.html California site for state tax forms and compliance.

www.edinfo.state.tx.us Good site for general business information and assistance.

www.irs.gov Site for Internal Revenue Service; tax forms and information.

www.tcs-libertylegal.com Site for Liberty Legal and corporate document books.

Other helpful sites not in the text:

www.accessincorp.com Access Incorporation Services; incorporation and business services for all fifty states.

www.fsb.com/guide The Fortune Small Business guide to helpful Internet sites for business start-up help. This has links to government statistical Web sites and other useful information.

http://entrepreneurship.mit.edu A one-week course in entrepreneurship is offered at the Sloan Graduate Business School at MIT. See other universities as well.

PART 2
FORMS FOR REQUIRED REPORTING OF TAXES AND PAYROLL

1. IRS Form 941: quarterly payroll tax deposit summary

2. IRS Form 940: annual federal unemployment tax reporting

3. Employer's quarterly report (state unemployment filing or SUTA report)

4. State sales and use tax report

5. Typical list of forms required by most state governments

6. List of helpful state publications

7. Summary list of major filings and dates or frequency of filing

IRS Form 941

Form **941 for 2005:** Employer's Quarterly Federal Tax Return   9501

(Rev. January 2005)   Department of the Treasury — Internal Revenue Service   OMB No. 1545-0029

Employer identification number ☐☐☐ — ☐☐☐☐☐☐☐

Name (not your trade name)

Trade name (if any)

Address

Number   Street   Suite or room number

City   State   ZIP code

Report for this Quarter ...
(Check one.)

☐ 1: January, February, March

☐ 2: April, May, June

☐ 3: July, August, September

☐ 4: October, November, December

Read the separate instructions before you fill out this form. Please type or print within the boxes.

Part 1: Answer these questions for this quarter.

1 Number of employees who received wages, tips, or other compensation for the pay period
including: *Mar. 12* (Quarter 1), *June 12* (Quarter 2), *Sept. 12* (Quarter 3), *Dec. 12* (Quarter 4)   **1**

2 Wages, tips, and other compensation **2**

3 Total income tax withheld from wages, tips, and other compensation **3**

4 If no wages, tips, and other compensation are subject to social security or Medicare tax . . ☐ Check and go to line 6.

5 Taxable social security and Medicare wages and tips:

		Column 1		Column 2
5a	Taxable social security wages		× .124 =	
5b	Taxable social security tips		× .124 =	
5c	Taxable Medicare wages & tips		× .029 =	

5d Total social security and Medicare taxes (*Column 2*, lines 5a + 5b + 5c = line 5d) . . **5d**

6 Total taxes before adjustments (lines 3 + 5d = line 6) **6**

7 Tax adjustments (If your answer is a negative number, write it in brackets.):

7a Current quarter's fractions of cents . . . .

7b Current quarter's sick pay . . . .

7c Current quarter's adjustments for tips and group-term life insurance

7d Current year's income tax withholding (Attach Form 941c) . . .

7e Prior quarters' social security and Medicare taxes (Attach Form 941c)

7f Special additions to federal income tax (reserved use) . . . . .

7g Special additions to social security and Medicare (reserved use)

7h Total adjustments (Combine all amounts: lines 7a through 7g.) **7h**

8 Total taxes after adjustments (Combine lines 6 and 7h.) **8**

9 Advance earned income credit (EIC) payments made to employees **9**

10 Total taxes after adjustment for advance EIC (lines 8 – 9 = line 10) **10**

11 Total deposits for this quarter, including overpayment applied from a prior quarter **11**

12 Balance due (lines 10 – 11 = line 12) Make checks payable to the *United States Treasury* . **12**

13 Overpayment (If line 11 is more than line 10, write the difference here.)   Check one ☐ Apply to next return.
         ☐ Send a refund.

Next ➡

For Privacy Act and Paperwork Reduction Act Notice, see the back of the Payment Voucher.   Cat. No. 17001Z   Form **941** (Rev. 1-2005)

9502

Name *(not your trade name)*	Employer identification number

Part 2: Tell us about your deposit schedule for this quarter.

If you are unsure about whether you are a monthly schedule depositor or a semiweekly schedule depositor, see *Pub. 15 (Circular E)*, section 11.

14 ☐ ☐ Write the state abbreviation for the state where you made your deposits OR write "MU" if you made your deposits in *multiple* states.

15 Check one: ☐ Line 10 is less than $2,500. Go to Part 3.

☐ You were a monthly schedule depositor for the entire quarter. Fill out your tax liability for each month. Then go to Part 3.

Tax liability: Month 1 [   ] .

Month 2 [   ] .

Month 3 [   ] .

Total [   ] .   Total must equal line 10.

☐ You were a semiweekly schedule depositor for any part of this quarter. Fill out *Schedule B (Form 941): Report of Tax Liability for Semiweekly Schedule Depositors*, and attach it to this form.

Part 3: Tell us about your business. If a question does NOT apply to your business, leave it blank.

16 If your business has closed and you do not have to file returns in the future . . . . ☐ Check here, and

enter the final date you paid wages [/   /   ] .

17 If you are a seasonal employer and you do not have to file a return for every quarter of the year . . ☐ Check here.

Part 4: May we contact your third-party designee?

Do you want to allow an employee, a paid tax preparer, or another person to discuss this return with the IRS? See the instructions for details.

☐ Yes. Designee's name [   ]

Phone ( ) − Personal Identification Number (PIN) ☐ ☐ ☐ ☐ ☐

☐ No.

Part 5: Sign here

Under penalties of perjury, I declare that I have examined this return, including accompanying schedules and statements, and to the best of my knowledge and belief, it is true, correct, and complete.

X

Sign your name here [   ]

Print name and title [   ]

Date [/   /   ]   Phone ( ) −

Part 6: For paid preparers only *(optional)*

Preparer's signature [   ]

Firm's name [   ]

Address [   ]   EIN [   ]

ZIP code [   ]

Date [/   /   ]   Phone ( ) −   SSN/PTIN [   ]

☐ Check if you are self-employed.

IRS Form 940

Form **940**	**Employer's Annual Federal Unemployment (FUTA) Tax Return**	OMB No. 1545-0028

Department of the Treasury
Internal Revenue Service (99)

▶ See the separate instructions for Form 940 for information on completing this form.

20 04

	T	
	FF	
	FD	
	FP	
	I	
	T	

You must complete this section. ▶

Name (as distinguished from trade name)   Calendar year

Trade name, if any   Employer identification number (EIN)

Address (number and street)   City, state, and ZIP code

A   Are you required to pay unemployment contributions to only one state? (If "No," skip questions B and C.)   ☐ Yes ☐ No

B   Did you pay all state unemployment contributions by January 31, 2005? ([1] If you deposited your total FUTA tax when due, check "Yes" if you paid all state unemployment contributions by February 10, 2005. (2) If a 0% experience rate is granted, check "Yes." (3) If "No," skip question C.) . . . .   ☐ Yes ☐ No

C   Were all wages that were taxable for FUTA tax also taxable for your state's unemployment tax? . . .   ☐ Yes ☐ No

D   Did you pay all wages in a state other than New York? . . . .   ☐ Yes ☐ No

If you answered "No" to any of these questions, you must file Form 940. If you answered "Yes" to all the questions, you may file Form 940-EZ, which is a simplified version of Form 940. (Successor employers, see **Special credit for successor employers** in the separate instructions.) You can get Form 940-EZ by calling 1-800-TAX-FORM (1-800-829-3676) or from the IRS website at **www.irs.gov.**

If you will not have to file returns in the future, check here (see **Who Must File** in the separate instructions) and complete and sign the return . . . . ▶ ☐

If this is an Amended Return, check here (see **Amended Returns** in the separate instructions) . . . . . ▶ ☐

Part I	**Computation of Taxable Wages**

1   Total payments (including payments shown on lines 2 and 3) during the calendar year for services of employees **1**

2   Exempt payments. (Explain all exempt payments, attaching additional sheets if necessary.) ▶ **2**

3   Payments of more than $7,000 for services. Enter only amounts over the first $7,000 paid to each employee (see separate instructions). Do not include any exempt payments from line 2. The $7,000 amount is the federal wage base. Your state wage base may be different. Do not use your state wage limitation **3**

4   Add lines 2 and 3 . . . .   **4**

5   Total taxable wages (subtract line 4 from line 1) . . . . ▶   **5**

6   Additional tax resulting from credit reduction for unpaid advances to the State of New York. Enter the wages included on line 5 for New York and multiply by .003. (See the separate instructions for Form 940.) Enter the credit reduction amount here and in Part II, line 5:
New York wages _____ x .003 = ... ▶   **6**

Be sure to complete both sides of this form, and sign in the space provided on the back.

For Privacy Act and Paperwork Reduction Act Notice, see separate instructions.   ▼ **DETACH HERE** ▼   Cat. No. 11234O   Form **940** (2004)

Form **940-V**	**Payment Voucher**	OMB No. 1545-0028

Department of the Treasury
Internal Revenue Service

Use this voucher only when making a payment with your return.

20 04

Complete boxes 1, 2, and 3. Do not send cash, and do not staple your payment to this voucher. Make your check or money order payable to the "United States Treasury." Be sure to enter your employer identification number (EIN), "Form 940," and "2004" on your payment.

1 Enter your employer identification number (EIN).	2 **Enter the amount of your payment.** ▶	Dollars	Cents
	3 Enter your business name (individual name for sole proprietors).		
	Enter your address.		
	Enter your city, state, and ZIP code.		

Form 940 (2004)   Page **2**

Name		Employer Identification number (EIN)

Part II   Tax Due or Refund

1	Gross FUTA tax. (Multiply the wages from Part I, line 5, by .062)	1	
2	Maximum credit. (Multiply the wages from Part I, line 5, by .054) . . | **2**		
3	Computation of tentative credit (**Note:** *All taxpayers must complete the applicable columns.*)		

(a) Name of state	(b) State reporting number(s) as shown on employer's state contribution returns	(c) Taxable payroll (as defined in state act)	(d) State experience rate period		(e) State experience rate	(f) Contributions if rate had been 5.4% (col. (c) x .054)	(g) Contributions payable at experience rate (col. (c) x col. (e))	(h) Additional credit (col. (f) minus col. (g)) If 0 or less, enter -0-.	(i) Contributions paid to state by 940 due date
			From	To					

3a	Totals . . . ▶		
3b	**Total tentative credit** (add line 3a, columns (h) and (i) only—for late payments, also see the instructions for Part II, line 4) . . . . ▶	3b	
4	**Credit:** Enter the smaller of the amount from Part II, line 2 or line 3b; or the amount from the worksheet on page 7 of the separate instructions	4	
5	Enter the amount from Part I, line 6	5	
6	**Credit allowable** (subtract line 5 from line 4). If zero or less, enter "-0-"	6	
7	**Total FUTA tax** (subtract line 6 from line 1). If the result is over $100, also complete Part III	7	
8	Total FUTA tax deposited for the year, including any overpayment applied from a prior year . .	8	
9	**Balance due** (subtract line 8 from line 7). Pay to the "United States Treasury." If you owe more than $100, see **Depositing FUTA Tax** on page 3 of the separate instructions . . . . . ▶	9	
10	**Overpayment** (subtract line 7 from line 8). Check if it is to be: ☐ **Applied to next return** or ☐ **Refunded** . . . . ▶	10	

Part III   **Record of Quarterly Federal Unemployment Tax Liability** (Do not include state liability.) **Complete only if line 7 is over $100.** See page 7 of the separate instructions.

Quarter	First (Jan. 1–Mar. 31)	Second (Apr. 1–June 30)	Third (July 1–Sept. 30)	Fourth (Oct. 1–Dec. 31)	Total for year
Liability for quarter					

Third-Party Designee	Do you want to allow another person to discuss this return with the IRS (see separate instructions)? ☐ **Yes.** Complete the following. ☐ **No**		
	Designee's name ▶	Phone no. ▶ ( )	Personal Identification number (PIN) ▶ ☐☐☐☐☐

Under penalties of perjury, I declare that I have examined this return, including accompanying schedules and statements, and, to the best of my knowledge and belief, it is true, correct, and complete, and that no part of any payment made to a state unemployment fund claimed as a credit was, or is to be, deducted from the payments to employees.

Signature ▶   Title (Owner, etc.) ▶   Date ▶

Form **940** (2004)

Employers Quarterly Report

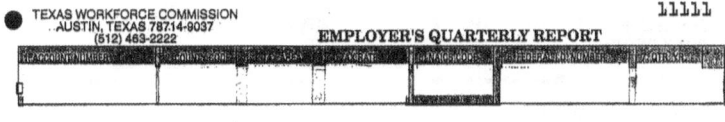

TEXAS WORKFORCE COMMISSION
AUSTIN, TEXAS 78714-9037
(512) 463-2222

EMPLOYER'S QUARTERLY REPORT

11111

ACCOUNT NUMBER	COUNTY CODE	WAGES	AGENT	GRADE CODE	FEDERAL ID NUMBER	RETURN PCT

8.

9. TELEPHONE NUMBER   06

	ALIGNMENT	9A. QUARTER ENDING	9B. PENALTIES WILL BE ASSESSED IF REPORT IS NOT POSTMARKED BY

1st Month   2nd Month   3rd Month

10. Enter in the boxes above the number of employees both full-time and part-time, in pay periods that include 12th day of the calendar month. (ENTER NUMERALS ONLY)

11. SHOW THE COUNTY CODE (see list on the back of C-4 form) in which you had the greatest number of employees.

12. If you have employees in more than one county in TEXAS, how many are outside the county shown in Item 11?

FILE AND PAY ONLINE
www.texasworkforce.org

	DOLLARS	CENTS
13. Total (Gross) Wages Paid During this Quarter to Texas Employees. (If none, enter "0")		
14. Taxable Wages paid this quarter to each employee up to $9000, the annual maximum amount. (If none, enter "0")		
15. Tax Due (Multiply Taxable Wages, Item 14, By Tax Rate, Item 4)		
16. Interest, If Tax is Past Due		
17. Penalty, If Report Is Past Due		
18. Balance Due From Prior Periods (Subtract Credit Or Add Debit)		
19. Total Due - Make Remittance Payable To TWC Please include payment voucher with remittance.		

14a. Mark box with an "X" if reporting wages to another state during the year for employees listed in Item 21.

FOR TWC USE ONLY

	MONTH	DAY	YEAR
POSTMARK DATE C3			
POSTMARK DATE $			
EX DATE C3			
EX DATE			

☐ Estimated

DOLLARS	CENTS	INITIALS

AMOUNT RECEIVED

	20. SOCIAL SECURITY NUMBER	1ST INIT	2ND INIT	21. EMPLOYEE NAME LAST NAME	22. TOTAL WAGES PAID THIS QUARTER
1					
2					
3					
4					
5					
6					
7					
8					
9					
10					

25. I DECLARE that the information herein is true and correct to the best of my knowledge and belief.

SIGNATURE_____

TITLE _____ DATE _____

PREPARERS NAME_____

PREPARERS PHONE NUMBER_____

For assistance in completing form call,

If you are unable to file and pay online, mail report and remittance to:
CASHIER
TEXAS WORKFORCE COMMISSION
P.O. BOX 149037
AUSTIN, TEXAS 78714-9037
DO NOT STAPLE REPORT

23. PAGE TOTAL	

FORM C - 3 (03/02)

24. MAKE CHANGES TO EMPLOYER INFORMATION USING **STATUS CHANGE FORM**. CHANGES NOTED ON THIS FORM MAY NOT BE CAPTURED DURING PROCESSING

State Sales and Use Tax Report

01-114
(Rev.1-05/34)   *** INTERNET ***   DDDD
b. ■

TEXAS SALES AND USE TAX RETURN

a. ■ 26100

c. Taxpayer number

SEE INSTRUCTIONS FORM 01-922

* *Do not staple or paper clip.*   * *Do not write in shaded areas.*   **Page 1 of**

d. Filing period

e.

f. Due date

g.   Taxpayer name and mailing address

* Blacken this box if your mailing address has changed. Show changes by the preprinted information.............. 1. ■
* Blacken this box if you are no longer in business. Write in the date you went out of business................................ 2. ■
* Blacken this box if one of your locations is out of business or has changed its address........................ 3. ■

You have certain rights under Ch. 559, Government Code, to review, request, and correct information we have on file about you. Contact us at the address or toll-free number listed on this form.

h. 8 8   i.

RETURN MUST BE FILED EVEN IF NO TAX IS DUE

l. **NO SALES** - If you had zero to report in Items 1, 2 and 3 for ALL locations for this filing period, blacken this box, sign and date this return and mail it ► to the Comptroller's office. 1

j. Are you taking credit to reduce taxes due on this return for taxes you paid in error on your own purchases? *(Blacken appropriate box)*..........   YES ☐ 1 ■   NO ☐ 2 ■

k. Did you refund sales tax for items exported outside the U.S. based on a Texas Licensed Customs Broker Export Certificate? *(Blacken appropriate box)*....   YES ☐ 1 ■   NO ☐ 2 ■

If you answered yes to either question j or k, you must complete Form 01-148 and submit it with your return.

PLEASE PRINT YOUR NUMERALS LIKE THIS   0 1 2 3 4 5 6 7 8 9

6. Physical location (outlet) name and address *(Do not use a P.O. box address.)*   Outlet no. ■

1. **TOTAL SALES** *(Whole dollars only)*.... ■

2. **TAXABLE SALES** *(Whole dollars only)*.... ■

3. **TAXABLE PURCHASES** *(Whole dollars only)*.... ■

4. Amount subject to state tax *(Item 2 plus Item 3)*.... ■

5. Amount subject to local tax *(Amount for city, transit, county and SPD must be equal.)* ■

7. **AMOUNT OF TAX DUE FOR THIS OUTLET** *(Dollars and cents)* *(Multiply "Amount subject to tax" by "TAX RATE" for state and local tax due)*

TAX RATES

X ■   =   7a. State tax *(Include in Item 8a)*

X ■   =   7b. Local tax *(Include in Item 8b)*

■ 26180   ■ STATE TAX - Column a   ■ LOCAL TAX - Column b

8. Total tax due *(from all outlets or list supplements)* ....

01-114
(Rev.1-05/34)   DDDD

9. Prepayment credit ....   –

10. Adjusted tax due *(Item 8 minus Item 9)*   =

11. TIMELY FILING DISCOUNT........................   –

12. Prior payments ....   –

13. Net tax due *(Item 10 minus Items 11 & 12)*....   =

14. Penalty and interest *(See instructions)*..............   +

15. **TOTAL STATE AND LOCAL AMOUNT DUE** *(Item 13 plus Item 14)*   =   ■

15a. Total state amount due

15b. Total local amount due

Mail to: COMPTROLLER OF PUBLIC ACCOUNTS
111 E. 17th Street
Austin, TX 78774-0100

■ T Code   ■ Taxpayer number

26020

■ Period

16. **TOTAL AMOUNT PAID** *(Total of Items 15a and 15b)*

n.

Taxpayer name

I declare that the information in this document and any attachments is true and correct to the best of my knowledge.
sign : Taxpayer or duly authorized agent   Date   Daytime phone (Area code & number)   Make check payable to:

Typical List of Forms Required by Most State Governments

Form:

C-198LR: Letter explaining the specific section of the law making you liable

C-22: Texas unemployment tax rate for your company

C-198R1: Employer statement of reports due

C-3: Employers quarterly report forms (can be filed via Internet)

C-4: Employers quarterly wages list (can be filed via Internet)

C-3V: Payment voucher

Y-10: Required employer poster

FL-160: Letter requesting status report (if none on file)

FL-1031: Letter requesting federal employer's ID number (if none on file)

List of Helpful State Publications

Texas Business Today **publication**

Workforce Solutions **brochure**

Office of the Attorney General New Hire **brochure**

More information is available at www.texasworkforce.org or similar sites in your state.

A similar list of forms for California can be found at www.taxes.ca.gov/forms1.html.

Summary List of Federal and State Filings and Frequencies

The following list is meant to help keep the new entrepreneur out of trouble with the state and federal governments. The filings required are complicated, and professional accounting help should be sought. There may be more forms required in your state.

Federal:

Form 8103, payroll withholding deposits	Monthly to start and then variable
Form 941, payroll tax deposits	Quarterly
Form 940, FUTA	Annually, and then variable
W2/W3, annual wage summary	Annually
Form 1065, partnership tax return (LLC)	Annually
or	
Form 1120, corporation tax return (Sub-S)	Annually
Form 1099 for vendors	Annually

State:

State unemployment deposits (SUTA)	Quarterly
Franchise or state income tax	Annually
State sales tax deposits	Monthly
Corporate status reports	Annually

Other:

Corporate record book: You should have quarterly meetings and record the proceedings in you record book. At least once a year you should have an equity owners' meeting and record all transactions and proceedings. This book must be kept up-to-date with ownership records to protect the company and equity holders.

PART 3
TYPICAL PROFIT AND LOSS STATEMENT (P&L) AND BUDGET COMPARISON

Typical Profit and Loss Statement (P&L)

	January 2006 Actual	Budget	A vs. B	Year to Date Actual	Budget	A vs. B
Total Sales	$541,516	$477,700	$63,816	$541,516	$477,700	$63,816
Raw Material Cost	262,995	224,081	-38,914	262,995	224,081	-38,914
Gross Profit	278,521	253,619	24,902	278,521	253,619	24,902
Expenses						
Variable						
Wages, regular	24,732	21,210	-3522	24,732	21,210	-3522
Wages, overtime	16,790	19,600	2810	16,790	19,600	2810
Payroll tax FICA	3,679	2,449	-1,230	3,679	2,449	-1,230
Payroll tax Medicare	204	673	470	204	673	470
Payroll tax FUTA	96	163	67	96	163	67
Payroll tax SUTA	81	16	-64	81	16	-64
Workers' compensation	0	0	0	0	0	0
Repairs and maintenance	3,121	9,353	6,231	3,121	9,353	6,231
Fuel (diesel)	10,316	10,077	-239	10,316	10,077	-239
Outside freight cost	24,270	11,500	-12,770	24,270	11,500	-12,770
Contract labor	888	8,600	7,712	888	8,600	7,712
Plant supplies	1,457	300	-1,157	1,457	300	-1,157
Utilities	1,774	1,200	-574	1,774	1,200	-574
Tolls	0	235	235	0	235	235
Office security	105	130	25	105	130	25
Disposal fees	283	270	-13	283	270	-13
$ G&A and Fixed						
Salaries	13,417	13,270	-147	13,417	13,270	-147
Payroll taxes salary	255	1,073	818	255	1,073	818
Employee medical insurance	3,121	1,670	-1,451	3,121	1,670	-1,451
Land lease	1,097	1,700	603	1,097	1,700	603
Office lease	1,181	450	-731	1,181	450	-731
Office expenses	3,095	800	-1,451	3,095	800	-1,451
Supplies	2,417	800	-1,617	2,417	800	-1,617
Telephone/internet	3,037	2,580	-457	3,037	2,580	-457
Postage	205	175	-30	205	175	-30
R&M office	3,093	2,380	-649	3,093	2,380	-649
Advertising	2,260	2,100	-160	2,260	2,100	-160
Travel	564	500	-64	564	500	-64
Meals/entertainment	557	275	-282	557	275	-282
Depreciation	14,357	14,925	569	14,357	14,925	569
Amortization	0	0	0	0	0	0
Interest expense	8,988	7,875	-1,113	8,988	7,875	-1,113
Research	8,400	10,000	1,600	8,400	10,000	1,600
Taxes, property	0	1,260	1,260	0	1,260	1,260
Professional fees	3,219	3,500	281	3,219	3,500	281
Insurance (liability)	3,449	3,850	401	3,449	3,850	401
Bank charges	209	495	287	209	495	287
Credit card charges	647	1,975	1,328	647	1,975	1,328
Miscellaneous	1,590	300	-1,290	1,590	300	-1,290
Bad debt	846	700	-146	846	700	-146
Total expenses	$163,971	$160,299	-$3,672	$163,971	$160,299	-$3,672
Net profit	$114,550	$93,320	$21,230	$114,550	$93,320	$21,230

Typical P&L format showing monthly results, year to date results and comparison to budgets

About the Author

Bruce C. Thornton has been described as a "serial entrepreneur," which sounds vaguely felonious. It actually means that he has had a penchant for starting businesses from an early age.

Mr. Thornton grew up in Houston Texas. He started an R&B band and became a semiprofessional musician (electric bass) while in high school. He also had a surfboard manufacturing company during high school years.

After earning a chemical engineering degree at the University of Texas at Austin, Mr. Thornton went to work for Arco Chemical, where he held various senior engineering and management positions. An early career in at a large company formed a good basis for understanding basic business functions. After Arco he left to begin the serial entrepreneurship phase.

Businesses founded and partially owned by Mr. Thornton include:

- Advanced Aromatics, Inc-produces petrochemicals and solvents in Baytown, TX. (President)
- Living Earth Technology, Inc-produces bulk and bagged horticultural and mulch products and is a major greenwaste recycler (now a division of Republic Services Group, RSG-NYSE). (President)
- CMS Technology, Inc-provides business development consulting and licenses chemical separation technology. (President)
- Growth Technology, Inc-manufactured and licensed natural and organic fertilizers. (Chairman)
- Swing Dynamics-manufactured split screen (two simultaneous views) portable video equipment to analyze golf swings. (Co-owner)
- Landscape Depot, LLC-manufactures bulk horticultural material in the Texas area. (Chairman)

- Advanced Laser Materials, LLC-Manufactures materials for rapid proto-typing (makes 3-dimensional objects using the laser-sintering process). (Chairman)

Mr. Thornton has served on many environmental and science advisory boards, and is currently an Entrepreneur-in-Residence at the University of Texas at Austin, where he volunteers time to assist engineering and technical students who want to start new businesses.

Other related activities:

University of Texas Engineering Foundation Advisory Council (director) and Chairman of the Commercialization Committee
Advisor to the UT Office of Technology Commercialization
Member of the Success Committee for the Clean Energy Incubator (part of Austin Technology Incubator)

Mr. Thornton and his wife Sharon live the in the Houston area in the winter and in Colorado Springs in the summer. He can be reached by e-mail at BCT_CMS@prodigy.net.

978-0-595-39262-9
0-595-39262-8